AUSTRALIA IN 22 DAYS

A STEP-BY-STEP GUIDE AND TRAVEL ITINERARY

BY JOHN GOTTBERG

In Fond Memory of the Blue Minx

This book would not have been possible without the assistance of the Australian Tourist Commission, the various state and territory tourist commissions, and the following individuals: Linda Carlock, Rick Steves, Ken Luboff, Richard Harris, Cesare Cataldo, Peggy Bendel, Elaine Kleckner, Craig Freeman, Patrick J. O'Reilly, Gina Dodd, John Greenslade, Sue Brennan, Carolyn Fitzpatrick, Don Knapp, Amanda Struthers, Gabby Smith, Scott Thornton, Bob Schatz, Julie and Kevin Keir, Bob and Greg Derwin, Linda and Alan Mulley, Margaret and John Bee.

Library of Congress Catalog No. 87-042773

Published by
John Muir Publications
Santa Fe, New Mexico
Printed in U.S.A.

22 Days series editor   Richard Harris
Design/Production   Mary Shapiro
Maps   Jim Wood
Cover   Tim Clark
Typography   Copygraphics, Inc.

ISBN 0-912528-75-3

CONTENTS

HOW TO USE THIS BOOK

G'day! In your hands is your fair dinkum, pocket-sized Aussie tour guide. It's designed for independent-minded blokes and birds who like the freedom and flexibility of going walkabout their own way, but who appreciate the efficiency that an organized tour offers.

Australia in 22 Days doesn't pretend to take you around the entire continent of "Oz" in three weeks. That would be like trying to see the whole United States in 22 days. It's a fair comparison: Australia is almost identical in size to the 48 contiguous states.

What I have tried to do in this itinerary is to provide a sampling of Australia's most fascinating features—from the great cities of Sydney and Melbourne, to predictable (and worthwhile!) tourist stops such as the Great Barrier Reef and Ayers Rock, to less known sites like reconstructed gold rush towns and an island of nesting penguins—and suggest how to appreciate them most thoroughly. I have done this in a manner to show how to get the maximum value for your travel dollar.

Because Australia is so vast, in order to see as much as possible within a three-week itinerary, you should rely on domestic airlines to cover large chunks of land between major attractions. Most of Australia's 16 million people live along the relatively fertile southeast coast, an area well-equipped with good roads and visitor facilities. The same is not true of the Outback. To get to the dry Centre from any direction, you are faced with a journey of many hundreds of miles across bleak, foreboding terrain. It is probably not a good idea to drive yourself there. Air travel, while no bargain, can save considerable time and worry. With extra time, much of the trip can be done by rental car or (more cheaply and reliably but with somewhat less freedom) by train and bus.

The trip outlined in this book begins in Sydney and concludes in Brisbane. International flights also serve Melbourne and Cairns, allowing you to start and end in any of these gateway cities. I suggest that you take an extra Friday off work and leave home on Thursday night, arriving in Sydney on Saturday morning to begin your adventure. This will make connections easier later in the trip (especially on the infrequent Alice Springs-Cairns air leg) and will allow you a full day to recover from jet lag at home before going back to work when your vacation's finished.

I like to compare any travel plan to a childhood Erector set. The itinerary should provide a framework for travel, but should not restrict the wanderer from indulging personal interests or whims. Take this itinerary and customize it to your own needs

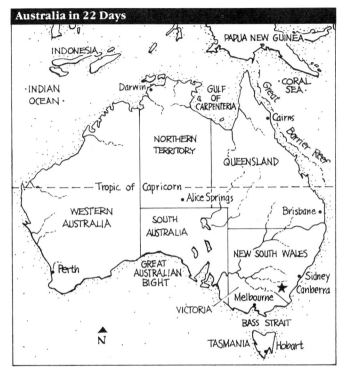

Australia in 22 Days

and wants. Make changes. Scribble in the margins. Cross things out; add new ones. Spend extra time in one place if it intrigues you, skip another if you find it boring. If there are things you'd like to do in Australia which I haven't listed in this book—by all means, do them.

Each chapter is modular in itself and can be included as part of whatever itinerary you yourself may want to develop. The 22 days are built with the same sections (though not always in this order):

1. An **Introductory Overview** of the day.
2. An hour-by-hour **Suggested Schedule** for the day.
3. A list of **Sightseeing Highlights** (rated: ▲▲▲Don't miss; ▲▲Try hard to see; ▲Worthwhile if you can make it).
4. **Orientation**, and an easy-to-read **map** of the area.
5. **Transportation** tips and instructions.
6. **Accommodations and Dining**: How and where to find the best places in your price range, including addresses, phone numbers and my favorites.
7. **Itinerary options** for those travelers with more or less than the suggested time, or with particular interests.

At the back of the book, I've included some optional tour extensions which expand on the main itinerary. You'll also find chapters presenting practical information and cultural insights to add to your appreciation of Australia.

In deciding when and where to launch your trip, consider holiday and event schedules and seasonal weather trends. January through March are the rainiest months along the northern Barrier Reef, for example, while June to September give the Snowy Mountains their name. Spring (October to mid-December) and autumn (mid-March to May) are the best months to cover all corners of this schedule.

Paperwork
To travel to Australia, you will need a valid passport and a tourist visa. Your tourist visa will cost you nothing except the price of a passport-sized photograph and a self-addressed stamped (and registered) envelope. Your travel agent can handle everything for you. Allow a couple of weeks for processing.

A tourist visa to Australia is typically good for up to six months, with multiple entries allowed for five years or the life of the passport. The tourist visa does prohibit you from working, seeking employment or taking a major course of study while you are in Australia. These require separate visas which must be obtained from outside the country.

Australian consular offices in the United States are located at:

1601 Massachusetts Ave. N.W., Washington, DC 20036 (tel. 202/797-3159)

636 5th Ave., New York, NY 10111 (tel. 212/245-4000)

111 E. Wacker Drive, Suite 2212, Chicago, IL 60601 (tel. 31²⁄₃29-1740)

1990 Post Oak Blvd., Suite 800, Houston, TX 77056 (tel. 713/629-9131)

611 N. Larchmont Blvd., Los Angeles, CA 90046 (tel. 213/380-0980)

360 Post St., San Francisco, CA 94108 (tel. 415/362-6165)

1000 Bishop St., Honolulu, HI 96813 (tel. 808/524-5050).

Offices in Canada are located at:

13th Floor, National Building, 130 Slater St., Ottawa, Ont. K1P 5H6 (tel. 613/236-0841)

Suite 2324 Commerce Court West, King and Bay Streets, Toronto, Ont. M5L 189 (tel. 416/367-0783)

1066 W. Hastings St., Vancouver, BC V6E 3X1 (tel. 604/684-1177).

Cost Considerations

Prices in Australian dollars for transportation, accommodation, food, etc., are roughly what you might expect to pay in the United States. The good news is that the Australian dollar is worth about 70 U.S. cents at this writing (May 1987), which means that when you're paying A$30 for a hotel room, you're actually only paying US$21. The same goes for restaurants, where you can pay A$8 for an excellent four-course dinner: in U.S. dollars you're actually only paying around US$5.60.

The prices estimated and quoted in this book are based on two people traveling together and sharing hotel rooms. If you're traveling alone, you can expect to spend somewhat more. If you're traveling with a larger group, it will cost you a bit less, especially when it comes to hotel rooms and taxi fares. The cost of meals and public transportation won't change much.

Excluding costs of air fares to and from Australia—about US$1,000 to US$1,200 from the U.S. West Coast—budget travelers can do this 22-day trip for around US$1,100. If this is you, you'll stay in hostel-style lodging for A$10 a night or less, travel by bus or train between Sydney and Melbourne, and spend A$600 for a 6,000-km airpass to fly the Melbourne-Alice Springs-Cairns-Brisbane legs of the trip. If it's not important to keep to the 22-day itinerary limit, you can shell out A$330 for a 22-day bus pass in lieu of the more expensive air pass— although your additional outlay for meals and accommodations will minimize the actual saving.

This trip is ideally suited and designed for the traveler with a little more money in his or her pocket—say, US$1,800 for the three-week journey, not including the getting there. If you are this middle-ground tourist, you'll spend an average of A$25 a night for a shared hotel room with private facilities, rent a car for the Sydney-Canberra-Melbourne highway leg, purchase an air pass and book the occasional tour, like a cruise to the outer Barrier Reef.

The traveler who likes to go everywhere in style, to stay at the best hotels and eat at the best restaurants, will also find this itinerary appropriate. You can do this within a budget of US$2,700 per person, splitting the cost of A$100-a-night hotel rooms, renting a car wherever you want, traveling on an air pass and booking numerous side tours and cruises during your visit.

The Australian dollar, by the way, is hard to find in paper these days. It's been replaced in everyday use by a A$1 gold-colored coin, leaping kangaroos on the flip side of Queen Elizabeth's portrait. Other coins are the heavy, 12-sided 50-cent piece, the 20-cent piece (slightly larger than an American quarter), the 10-cent piece (similar in size to a dime), the 5-cent piece (about like a Canadian 5-center), the 2-cent piece (copper, bigger than a penny) and the 1-cent penny (much like ours). Paper money, from the lime-green A$2 note to the blue-gray A$100, grows in size and changes color as denominations increase. (In between are $5, $10, $20, and $50 notes.)

It is safest to carry your U.S. dollars in the form of travelers checks, which you can exchange at city banks 9:30 a.m. to 4 p.m. Monday to Thursday, 9:30 a.m. to 5 p.m. Friday and at airport currency counters or major hotel desks anytime.

When to Go
Australia's big tourist season is during the school holidays which fall in the middle of summer, appropriately—December, January and into February. This is the warmest time of year Down Under, but for four very good reasons, this is NOT a time of year when I would recommend going to Australia:

(1) This is when the Australians are on holiday. You'll find most attractions as well as accommodations heavily booked, and there's a lot of competition to get hold of rental cars, which tends to drive prices up a bit.

(2) This is the rainy season in north Queensland; indeed, it's sometimes the cyclone season. Torrents of rain fall in the northern Barrier Reef (Cairns-Townsville) area, especially from January to March. Don't go without your brolly (umbrella).

(3) Blowflies—some call them the Australian national bird—are vicious anytime in the Outback, but especially under the hot summer sun.

(4) Perhaps most of all, December through March are classified as "high season" by international airlines, which jack up their fares 35% to 50% during this period. You can add a minimum of US$360 to your round-trip air fare if you insist on traveling at this time.

June, July and August, the North American summer but the Australian winter, are superb in the tropics and subtropics, but the further south you go, the less pleasant you're likely to find the weather. Melbourne, for example, whose climate is comparable to San Francisco, can easily have four seasons in a day. What's more, as you travel through Canberra into the Snowy Mountains, you're almost guaranteed to run into snow, and that may cause the closure of some roads.

In my estimation, the ideal times for travel in Australia are autumn (mid-March through May) and spring (September to November). On average, the climate is the best at that time in all parts of the country, and you won't be fighting for rooms like you might be during the peak summer season.

What to Bring
As little as possible. Traveling light frees you from the trials of
vagabondage to enjoy your journey more thoroughly.

Unless you're in Oz in the winter or are prone to straying into
higher elevations, you shouldn't need anything warmer than a
sweater and possible a rainjacket. Cairns, in far north
Queensland, is at the same latitude south as Guatemala is north,
and it's equally as tropical. The southernmost point on the
Australian continent, near Melbourne, if flipped across the
Equator would be no further north than Washington, D.C., or
Lake Tahoe.

Tend toward lighter clothes, wash-and-wear items that you
can wash in your hotel room and dry overnight. I take what I
wear and two more sets of everything. Some say I overpack.
Australia is a very informal country, and unless you plan to do
business on Collins Street in Melbourne (the only city in
Australia where a coat and tie are almost prerequisite), you'll be
fine in any situation with a long-sleeved shirt and slacks, or a
plain top and wrap-around skirt.

If you're going to use them, bring a camera and lenses (as few
as necessary). Buy your film in Australia. You'll want sunglasses
for the beaches and the desert; if you get to the Outback and
discover you need a wide-brimmed hat with character, choose
one there. A good pair of walking shoes is essential. Of course,
one thing you should never travel without is a sense of humor.

Flying to Australia
The cheapest fares from North America are from the West Coast
gateway cities of Los Angeles, San Francisco and Vancouver
(Canada). It is occasionally possible to find cut-rate or charter
tickets for as little as US$800 round-trip. During the April-
through-November "low season," you should plan on spending
US$950, perhaps up to US$1,100, for an APEX (advance purchase excursion) fare. From December to March, Australia's
"high season," a round-trip APEX fare can run US$1,300 to
US$1,500.

Trans-Pacific flights leave the West Coast between 8 and 11
p.m., arriving in Sydney a day and a half later (after crossing the
International Date Line) sometime between 6 and 9 a.m. Qantas, the Australian national flag carrier, flies daily from both San
Francisco and Los Angeles, often with stopovers in Honolulu or
Tahiti. Nightly service is also offered by Air New Zealand from
Los Angeles to Auckland and Sydney via Tahiti or Honolulu
and/or Fiji; by United Air Lines from L.A. to Sydney, nonstop or
via Honolulu; and by Continental Airlines from San Francisco
and L.A. Canadian Pacific Airlines flies twice weekly from Vancouver to Sydney via Honolulu and/or Fiji, while UTA French

Airlines has weekly services from Los Angeles to Sydney via
Tahiti, Auckland and Noumea, New Caledonia.

Flights originating from the U.S. East Coast are routed
through either of the California cities. It's also possible to connect in Great Britain or Europe with Australia-bound flights of
Qantas, British Airways, Lufthansa, KLM Dutch Airlines, Air
India, Cathay Pacific, Singapore Airlines and others.

Sydney is 18 hours ahead of the U.S. West Coast, 15 hours
ahead of New York and the East Coast. When you travel west
across the Pacific, you're crossing the International Date Line,
so you lose a day. Not to worry, the Aussies would say. She'll be
right. You'll pick up that day coming home again.

Of course, if you keep moving west, you won't pick up that
day. That's something to consider: for US$2,500, roughly twice
the amount of your round-trip ticket, you could fly around the
world. For US$2,000, you could invest in a circle-Pacific fare
and take in Asia. Read more about those options in *Asia
Through the Back Door*, authored by Rick Steves and yours
truly, also published by John Muir Publications.

Getting Around in Australia
As I mentioned earlier, within the context of this three-week
itinerary, it is most efficient to fly across large chunks of other-
wise tedious territory. The cost-wise way to do this is to purchase a reduced-fare air pass.

Your best bet is Ansett Airlines' "Go Australia Airpass,"
available through your travel agent before you leave home or
from an Ansett office within 30 days of your arrival in Australia.
For A$600 (US$390), you can travel up to 6,000 kilometers with
as many as five stopovers. The flight segments recommended in
this itinerary total 5,617 km.

If you can't leave Australia without making a pilgrimage to the
site of Dennis Conner's 1987 America's Cup victory in Fremantle, near Perth, you'll need to upgrade to Ansett's A$950
(US$665) pass, allowing 10,000 km and eight stopovers.

That the pass is a bargain is beyond doubt. Without the air
pass, you'd be paying close to A$900 for this book's Melbourne-
Ayers Rock-Alice Springs-Cairns-Brisbane excursion. (Be sure
to have your travel agent book your seat on these segments well
in advance.)

Ansett is one of two major domestic carriers in Australia. The
other, Australian Airlines, is every bit as good. For our purposes,
though, there's one significant difference: Ansett has the sole
concession on Alice Springs-to-Ayers Rock air travel. Australian
Airlines has a routing edge only in flights to outback
Queensland.

Two other transportation pass options may interest budget

travelers—bus and train. Three separate motorcoach firms with extensive national routes offer passes for unlimited travel within their city-to-city express systems. Deluxe Coachlines, the "Avis" ("we try harder") of the three, has a "Koalapass" valid for 10 to 90 days. (A 15-day pass is A$240, a 22-day pass A$330, a 62-day pass A$670.) Greyhound has passes for 14 (A$250) to 60 (A$690) days, while Ansett Pioneer's "Aussiepass" is valid for 15 (A$260) to 60 (A$690) days. Ansett advertises free city sightseeing in some cities, discount tours in others, for passholders. Discount motel packages are also available in concert with the coach passes.

Railways of Australia have an "Austrailpass" valid for unlimited first-class travel, and a "Budget Austrailpass" for unlimited economy travel, on its route system. (This system is limited: The only way to travel from Alice Springs to Cairns is via Sydney.) The minimum duration is 14 days (A$440 first-class, A$290 budget); one month is A$450 budget, three months cost A$730 budget. There's an additional charge for overnight berths (A$20 Brisbane-Cairns, for example; A$33 Adelaide-Alice Springs; A$99 Melbourne-Perth).

My major objection to travel by train or bus is that they carry you only from urban area to urban area. You don't see rural Australia except through smoked windows. Buses and trains pass through an area only two or three times daily; if you want to disembark and take a closer look at something interesting, you're going to have a long wait before the next coach shoots through. You wouldn't even get to the exquisite Victorian gold town of Beechworth; the main-line buses don't go there. And how could you possibly do a wine-tasting tour of Australia's great vineyard districts by bus or train?

Renting a Car and Driving
The best way to see southeastern Australia is to drive your own vehicle. A car allows you much more freedom in your travels, plus an opportunity to get in touch with the "real" Australia. Part of this 22-day tour is geared for the car traveler. If two of you, or better yet, four are traveling together, you'll share the costs of the vehicle and really cut your expenses.

To rent a car in Australia, you must be over 21 years old, preferably have a major credit card, and definitely have a valid driver's license. It is not necessary for you to have an international driver's license. A valid license from any state or Canadian province is quite sufficient.

All major airports have a handful of rental agencies: many are also located in central city areas near major hotels. In Sydney, check the rental agencies on William Street between downtown and King's Cross. While Hertz and Avis are the old standbys, you'll probably get a better rate from Thrifty or from any number of smaller, locally owned firms.

Plan on an outlay of A$45 to A$55 a day (about US$32 to US$39), including limited kilometers. Petrol (gas), in New South Wales and Victoria priced at 50 to 55 Australian cents a liter (US$1.33 to US$1.46 a gallon), will be your only other major driving expense. (The cost of petrol is slightly cheaper in South Australia and southeastern Queensland, a bit higher in Tasmania and Western Australia.)

Remember that Australia, like most nations of the world, employs the metric system of measurement. There are roughly 3.8 liters to one U.S. gallon. Eight kilometers equal about five miles.

Your major adjustment driving in Australia rather than North America is that you will be driving a right-hand drive car on the left-hand side of the road. This is not as difficult as you might at first imagine. Everything is simply reversed. Just remember to keep the center line next to the steering wheel, just as you would back home. (But in Australia it's on your right, not on your left.) Your major difficulty may be in turning. Be sure to stay in the left-hand lane: avoid turning across traffic to the right side of the road.

In the cities you don't need a car, and shouldn't use one. It's not worth the frustration, between rush-hour traffic, parking hassles and confusing local laws. (Downtown Melbourne, for instance, requires drivers to pull all the way to the left of an intersection and wait for traffic to clear before turning *right*.) Inner city public transportation is very good. Buses, Sydney subways and Melbourne trams are all excellent. Taxis are moderately priced. Turn your car in on arrival in a new city and save yourself many headaches.

"Petrol" isn't the only new word you'll have to learn for driving Down Under. Your car does not have a trunk and a hood; it has a boot and a bonnet. The windshield is known as the windscreen. You don't pass other vehicles; you overtake them. Roads aren't paved; they're sealed, or covered with bitumen. In cities, pavement is what you find across the kerb (curb) on the footpath (sidewalk).

The only roads in Australia that are really in good condition are the main highways—particularly the Sydney-to-Melbourne Hume Highway, a four-lane thoroughfare. Many other roads are in less than optimum shape, sealed but with no shoulders and with lots of ruts and potholes.

Those signs warning of "Next 10 km" of kangaroos or other Aussie animals should be more than curiosities, especially to night drivers. You won't often see wild animals in the daytime, but please drive carefully after dark.

Where to Stay
Australia has a real choice here, with accommodations of all
standards at all price levels.

I rate budget accommodations as those costing A$15 and less
a night; economy A$15 to A$40, moderate A$40 to A$80 and
deluxe over A$80. There are a number of categories to
consider.

Hotels run the full gamut from the internationally ranked
Regent of Sydney all the way down to the corner pub with a
few basic rooms in the attic. Deluxe to economy.

Private hotels are not licensed to sell liquor, and therefore
are usually lower in cost. Moderate and economy.

Guest houses are private hotels that provide bed and
breakfast, often (but not always) included in the tariff. Moderate
and economy.

Self-catering apartments are, in essence, hotel suites with
their own cooking facilities, and sometimes private laundry
facilities. Deluxe and moderate.

Motels in Australia offer much the same as their American
counterparts. Deluxe to economy.

Hostels may or may not be members of the International
Youth Hostel Federation. IYH member hostels are located in
cities, towns and national parks throughout the country. Private
"backpackers hostels" with similar price structures are more
recent developments in major cities and tourist centers. Budget.

Caravan parks are not only for caravans (what Americans
call "trailers"). You can set up a tent or, in many cases, stay in a
small housekeeping cabin with a hotplate. Budget.

Farm holidays will place you on a "station" far from the
bright city lights, where you can watch the dogs muster the
sheep—or help a jackeroo round up his cattle by helicopter.
Write: 9 Fletcher St., Woollahra, Sydney, NSW 2025, for details.
Moderate and economy.

What and Where to Eat and Drink
Australia is a very cosmopolitan country. This is especially true
in Sydney and Melbourne, which have very large populations of
south Europeans, Lebanese and Asians. Nowhere is their
influence felt more strongly than in the variety and quality of
reasonably priced cuisine. You can eat well at any meal for
under A$10. If you plan to spend A$20 per day per person on
food, you're perhaps being a little bit extravagant—or else you're
budgeting for an occasional splurge at a classier restaurant.

Though not widely acknowledged, there *is* an Australian
cuisine somewhat more imaginative than the bland British and
Irish cooking from which it derived. Aussie "tucker" comprises
the like of occasionally palatable dishes such as kangaroo tail

soup, meat pies, "snags" (large sausages), damper (unleavened campfire bread) and Vegemite (a strong-tasting yeast bread); and more delectable delicacies like carpetbagger steak (tenderloin stuffed with Sydney rock oysters), roast lamb in mint sauce, pavlova (a meringue dessert), and superb seafood—yabbies (a small lobster), Moreton Bay bugs (another small crustacean), Tasmanian scallops, and indigenous fish like barramundi, jewfish and John Dory.

I will typically begin my day in Australia with a light breakfast of fresh fruit—pawpaws (papayas) and mangoes are always in season—and/or pastry with a cup of tea or coffee. Later in the morning I might stop for Devonshire tea, served with fresh scones (with whipped cream and strawberry jam).

For lunch, I might pick up some fish and chips or a chicko roll at the takeaway counter of a milk bar (sort of like a 7-11 with a fast food counter). More often, I'll pause for pub grub. You never really go wrong if you go to eat in a pub. The price is right—often A$4 to A$6 for a full meal—and you can pick some pretty good meals off the blackboard menu: roast chicken, grilled fish, steak-and-kidney pie, even cook your own T-bone.

At dinnertime, I'll often head off to the European or Asian section of town, read the menus posted in the windows and wander in where I see the locals eating. And I almost always wash it down with a glass of good Aussie beer or wine. Many restaurants acclaim themselves as "BYO": bring your own alcoholic beverage. They may charge a small corkage fee, but their prices are almost always lower than licensed restaurants, and it's no great incovenience to stop by the bottle shop at a nearby pub (pub = "public hotel").

Beer is the Australian national drink, and it certainly deserves that distinction. Those who compile such statistics say the Aussies drink more beer per capita—some 30 gallons annually—than anyone but the Bavarians and Belgians. Every state has its own breweries and is stubbornly proud of its local brews. Drink from middies or pots (10-ounce glasses) or from schooners (15 ounces).

Australian wine has become recognized as among the best in the world. The principal growing areas are the Barossa Valley, focused on Tanunda northeast of Adelaide, and the Hunter Valley, around Cessnock north of Sydney. Victoria and Western Australial also have excellent wineries. Riesling, semillon, chardonnay and white burgundy are among the better white wines; in the reds, consider claret, cabernet sauvignon, shiraz and merlot.

Information Sources
This slender tome is not intended to be more than a travel planner used in conjunction with a more complete guidebook.

Lonely Planet's *Australia: A Travel Survival Kit*, by Tony Wheeler et al., has long been the bible of shoestring travelers in Australia, and deservedly so. The book has grown to become a very comprehensive volume of some 400 pages thoroughly covering the entire continent. It is a book that no traveler, especially no budget traveler, should go without. An option, not as detailed nationwide but reasonably good in the major cities, is Frommer's *Australia on $25 a Day* by John Godwin. For middle and upper-income travelers looking to get the most quality for their dollar, I highly recommend W. Bone's *Maverick Guide to Australia* (Gretna, La.: Pelican). An excellent book for planning your trip, and as a souvenir when your trip is over, is Apa Productions' lavishly illustrated *Insight Guide: Australia*. You should be able to find any of these books at major bookshops across North America.

In planning, don't overlook the assistance you can get from the Australian Tourist Commission and from the individual state and territory tourist boards. They can provide an enormous amount of valuable information for your journey. They also can provide the best highway maps I've found on Australia and its separate states. It's all free, and all commissions have offices in North America:

Australian Tourist Commission
489 Fifth Ave., New York, NY 10017 (tel. 212/687-6300)
3550 Wilshire Blvd., Suite 1740, Los Angeles, CA 90010 (tel. 213/380-6060)
120 Eglinton Ave. E., Suite 220, Toronto, Ont. M4P 1E2 (tel. 416/487-2126).

New South Wales Tourist Commission
2049 Century Park East, Suite 2250, Los Angeles, CA 90067 (tel. 213/552-9566).

Northern Territory Tourism Commission
3550 Wilshire Blvd., Suite 1610, Los Angeles, CA 90010 (tel. 213/383/7092).

Queensland Tourist and Travel Corporation
489 Fifth Ave., 31st Floor, New York, NY 10017 (tel. 687-6300)
3550 Wilshire Blvd., Suite 1738, Los Angeles, CA 90010 (tel. 213/381-3062)
890 W. Pender St., Suite 600, Vancouver, BC V6C 1J9 (tel. 604/687-7975).

South Australian Department of Tourism
3550 Wilshire Blvd., Suite 1740, Los Angeles, CA 90010 (tel. 213/380-5422).

Tasmanian Department of Tourism
   3550 Wilshire Blvd., Suite 1740, Los Angeles, CA 90010 (tel.
213/380-6060).
Victorian Tourism Commission
   3550 Wilshire Blvd., Suite 1736, Los Angeles, CA 90010 (tel.
213/387-3111).
Western Australian Tourism Commission
   489 Fifth Ave., New York, NY 10017 (tel. 212/687-1442)
   3550 Wilshire Blvd., Los Angeles, CA 90010 (tel.
213/383-7122).

Other Reading
Nearly all Aussies identify with the Outback, the "bush," even if
they are (as are most) urban dwellers. To get a feeling for this
tradition, I would go back to the short stories and poetry of
19th Century writers Henry Lawson and A.B. "Banjo" Paterson.
Lawson is more highly acclaimed in Australia, though Paterson's
ballads—"Waltzing Matilda," "The Man from Snowy River" —
are better known to Americans.
   The best Australian novel in recent years is Colleen
McCullough's *The Thorn Birds*. Some North Americans know
the mini-series (starring Richard Chamberlain) better than the
book. A young Aussie writer who impresses me is Tim Winton
(*That Eye, the Sky*).
   Good histories are Donald Horne's *The Australian People:
Biography of a Nation* and F.R. Crowley's *A New History of
Australia*. Robert Hughes' superb *The Fatal Shore* (1987) deals
with Australia's convict history and, indirectly, its impact on the
modern nation. For a better understanding of aboriginal history
and culture, see *Australian Dreaming* edited by Jennifer Isaacs.
Titles by Michael Morcombe and Eric Worrell are among the
best dealing with Australia's rich natural history.

Write Me a Letter
Change affects Australia as it does everywhere in the world. No
matter how hard I try to keep this book up to date, there's
always going to be something I miss. If this volume helps you
enjoy your trip, if it doesn't help you, if you've found things
which need more explanation, if you've found things which
would add to the enjoyment of other travelers, I would love to
hear from you. Please send your tips and recommendations,
love mail and hate mail, criticism and corrections, c/o John
Muir Publications, P.O. Box 613, Santa Fe, NM 87504. In return
for ideas used, I'll send you a free copy of my next edition.
   Meanwhile—happy travels!

ITINERARY

Whenever I mention to an Australian that I'm the author of a book titled "Australia in 22 Days," I'm greeted first with a dazed look, then a chuckle: "Oh, you'd be buggered after that one, mate!" they say as they shout another beer. But the fact remains that most Americans have only, if they're lucky, three weeks of vacation in which to see Australia. So here is my suggested itinerary, which I hope provides the best sampling of the country in a limited period of time. I encourage you to add days for relaxation whenever possible, because the pace of travel—over 4,000 miles in a very short time—can be exhausting.

Here is an overview of the 22-day itinerary:

DAY 1 (Saturday) Arrive in Sydney in the morning, get set up in your accommodation, then enjoy an afternoon cruise on beautiful Sydney Harbour. Call it quits right after dinner tonight, cheating jet lag with an early bedtime.

DAY 2 (Sunday) The Sydney Explorer bus will escort you to all major city sights for one set fare. Highlights will include the famous Opera House; the Australian Museum; and The Rocks, Sydney's oldest neighborhood. Enjoy an atmospheric dinner at the Argyle Tavern in The Rocks, with bush ballad sing-alongs.

DAY 3 (Monday) Exercise your options. I like to start the day at Bondi Beach, then visit the colonial Vaucluse House mansion and wander through the suburbs of Double Day and Paddington. If it's marsupials you want to see, take the ferry across the harbour to Taronga Park Zoo, and include a visit to Manly, with its famous surf beach and Marineland. History buffs may want to visit Old Sydney Town in Gasford; oenophiles should make a side trip to the Hunter Valley. Spend the night at Kings Cross, where you can play or gape at others playing.

DAY 4 (Tuesday) Pick up your reserved rental car in Sydney early this morning, with plans to leave it in Melbourne in a week. After a stop to see the working sheep farm at Gledswood homestead, continue to historic Berrima for lunch. On arrival in Canberra, visit the Regatta Point Planning Exhibition to understand the design and evolution of this modern capital, then drive to the top of Mount Ainslie for a good overview.

DAY 5 (Wednesday) Explore Canberra. Start at the Parliament House, if possible watching the House of Representatives or Senate in session from a public gallery. Take a drive through the Yarralumla area to see the impressive row of national embassies,

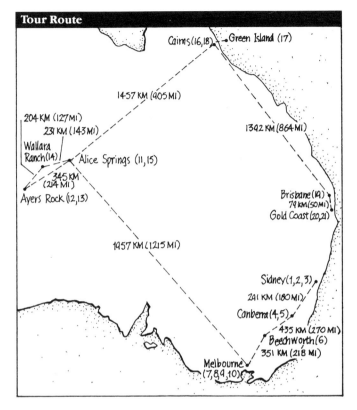

Tour Route

Cairns (16,18)   Green Island (17)

1457 KM (905 MI)

204 KM (127 MI)
231 KM (143 MI)   1392 KM (864 MI)

Wallara
Ranch (14)   Alice Springs (11,15)

345 KM
(214 MI)
Ayers Rock (12,13)   Brisbane (19)
                                                     79 KM (50 MI)
                                                     Gold Coast (20,21)

1957 KM (1215 MI)

                                            Sidney (1,2,3)
                                            291 KM (180 MI)
                                     Canberra (4,5)
                                            435 KM (270 MI)
                                            Beechworth (6)
                                            351 KM (218 MI)
                              Melbourne
                              (7,8,9,10)

then lunch at the High Court, inspect the National Gallery and
visit the Australian War Memorial museum.

DAY 6 (Thursday) There's a long day of driving ahead, so get
an early start. Today's route leads past the alpine resort of
Thredbo in the Snowy Mountains, and via Corryong, reputed
home of poet Banjo Paterson's "Man from Snowy River," to
Beechworth, a town straight out of the 19th Century gold-rush
era.

DAY 7 (Friday) After a morning look at Beechworth, visit
the Brown Brothers Winery, one of Australia's finest, and stop
in Glenrowan, where Ned Kelly, Australia's most notorious 19th
Century bushranger, made his "last stand." The afternoon's
highlight is the Sir Colin McKenzie Wildlife Sanctuary at
Healesville, an open-air reserve that is the best of its kind in the
world. You'll reach Melbourne in time for dinner.

DAY 8 (Saturday) Explore Melbourne today. Wander through its ethnic neighborhoods, its sophisticated shopping arcades, its high-brow business district. Don't miss the beautiful Victorian Arts Centre or the nation's best botanic gardens. The Old Gaol and the National Museum are worthy stops. But don't overdo the sightseeing. Here in sports-crazy Melbourne, you should soak up some Australian culture with (depending on the season) a visit to a "footie" match, a cricket test or a horse race.

DAY 9 (Sunday) Drive to Ballarat, site of Australia's greatest gold rush and its most famous rebellion. The Sovereign Hill theme park realistically recreates the town's heyday. The adjacent Gold Museum and the Eureka Exhibition memorialize Eureka Stockade, the nation's 1854 reply to Bunker Hill. Return to Melbourne in the late afternoon.

DAY 10 (Monday) Drive east into the Dandenong Ranges, where you can wonder at William Ricketts' unique forest sculptures, search for Lyrebirds in Sherbrooke Forest, or take a ride on the Puffing Billy. Proceed to Phillip Island, where fairy penguins parade from the sea at dusk. Then return to Melbourne.

DAY 11 (Tuesday) Drop your car at Melbourne's Tullamarine airport and catch a morning flight to Alice Springs. You'll have all afternoon and evening to explore this Outback oasis. Stop by the Old Telegraph Station, the Royal Flying Doctor Service and the Aboriginal art galleries. Climax your day with something unique: Ride a camel down the dry Todd River bed to dinner at a desert winery.

DAY 12 (Wednesday) Marvel at the weird geology of the Red Centre as you fly from Alice Springs to Yulara resort village at Ayers Rock, arriving in the early afternoon. After getting settled in your lodging and exploring the community, join the sunset barbecue tour to The Olgas.

DAY 13 (Thursday) Learn about the Aboriginal culture today. Spend the morning with a native guide who will show you how his people found food, water, shelter and medicine in this arid landscape. Visit the craft exhibit at the Uluru National Park ranger station and search for ancient petroglyphs in caves around the base of Ayers Rock. Back at Yulara, sip champagne as you watch the sun set over the red rock. Turn in early, because tomorrow, if you're energetic, you will . . .

DAY 14 (Friday) . . . climb The Rock. If the world's largest monolith is awesome at sunset, it's even more stunning at dawn. Awaken early to watch the light change its appearance, and to beat the heat and flies as you scale the huge red rock so that you, too, can wear a T-shirt declaring: "I Climbed Ayers Rock." Then board a bus for the 125-mile drive to the Wallara Ranch, where you'll spend the night at an Outback station.

DAY 15 (Saturday) Scramble through the sheer walls of colorful Kings Canyon, then return to Alice Springs in the evening. If you're not exhausted, enjoy a nightcap at the casino.

DAY 16 (Sunday) A travel day, Alice Springs to Cairns. On arrival in Cairns, the humidity will tell you immediately that you are in the tropics. Have a cold beer at an Esplanade pub and watch the fishing and pleasure boats come and go to the Great Barrier Reef. For dinner, order barramundi, a delectable river-run reef cod.

DAY 17 (Monday) Ship out for Green Island, a tiny coral enclave 40 minutes' cruise offshore where you can swim, study the sea life from a glass-bottom boat, view the largest crocodile in captivity in the world, and dine, drink and sleep at the small resort.

DAY 18 (Tuesday) You'll leave Green Island this morning to spend the day snorkeling or diving on the outer Barrier Reef. This experience should not be missed. More than 200 species of tropical reef fish can be seen swimming through a fantastic undersea "garden" of multicolored coral. Return to Cairns at night.

DAY 19 (Wednesday) The scenic Kuranda Railway will take you inland to the edge of the rainforested Atherton Tableland, climbing steeply above fields of sugar cane to the Barron River Gorge. In Kuranda, you'll have time to see Barron Falls, the open-air market and the Noctarium before returning to Cairns after lunch. Take a late afternoon flight to Brisbane.

DAY 20 (Thursday) Brisbane's No. 1 tourist sight is the Lone Pine Koala Sanctuary, Australia's largest. If you ever wanted a photo of yourself holding one of these seemingly cuddly creatures, here's where to have it taken. Travel there by boat up the Brisbane River. (In 1988, you may want to spend an extra day in Brisbane at Expo 88.) After lunch, take a bus to the Gold Coast, Australia's version of Miami Beach. Catch the day's last rays on the beach.

DAY 21 (Friday) Your final day on Australian beaches. The Gold Coast's biggest town is called Surfers Paradise; why not decide for yourself if the name really fits? Or you can dive into tourist attractions like Sea World, the Currumbin Bird Sanctuary or the Mudgeeraba Boomerang Factory.

DAY 22 (Saturday) It's been a great 22 days. Board your flight home to the States in Brisbane this afternoon. You'll reach the U.S. West Coast only 1½ hours after leaving Australia, thanks to the International Date Line. The longest day of your life was custom-made for savoring those great Australian memories.

DAY 1
ARRIVE IN SYDNEY

Welcome to Australia! This is your first day Down Under, but
you have many more to come, so don't exhaust yourself too
quickly. You will arrive in Sydney in the morning. After clearing
customs and immigration, travel into the city, get set in your
hotel, refresh yourself, then spend the afternoon on a leisurely
cruise of the beautiful Sydney Harbour.

Suggested Schedule

6:30-9:30 a.m.	Arrive at Sydney Airport.
7:30-10:30 a.m.	Take a bus into the city.
8:15-11:15 a.m.	Get set up in your accommodation.
12:30 p.m.	Lunch.
2:00 p.m.	Sydney Harbour "Coffee Cruise" from Circular Quay. Or take a ferry to Manly.
5:00 p.m.	Return to hotel.
6:30 p.m.	Dinner in Darlinghurst.
9:00 p.m.	Collapse into bed.

Airport Orientation

Kingsford Smith (Sydney) International Airport is located about
10 km south of the city centre on Botany Bay. (Start thinking in
metrics as soon as you arrive: 10 kilometers is about six miles.)
When your plane drops in over the bay, you'll be arriving Down
Under at almost the exact place as did Captain James Cook, the
first European to visit Australia, in 1770. Unlike Cook, you'll
have to clear immigration and customs. Cap'n Jim was fortunate
not to have to go through those formalities two centuries ago.

Travelers unlucky enough to arrive at the same time as a half-
dozen other international flights will disagree, but I've always
found the immigration procedures relatively painless here.
Hopefully, you'll zoom through quite quickly, wait a few
minutes to pluck your luggage from the baggage carousels, then
move straight through customs into the arrival hall.

Change some money into Australian dollars at the airport
bank, to the right. The rate here isn't quite as good as you'll find
at the banks in the city, but the hotel counters are open to meet
all incoming international flights; and if you've followed my
suggestion and arrived on a Saturday, you'll need enough cash

to get you through the weekend. (At this writing, I was getting A\$1.38 to US\$1 at the airport, A\$1.40 in town. Incidentally, some banks charge as much as A\$5 commission for transactions; others assess no commission. Inquire before you exchange.)

At the south end of the arrival hall (furthest from the bank) is the Travellers Information Service desk. Here you can obtain hotel reservations, maps, information on tourist attractions in Sydney, and book a shuttle bus ticket into town. A bus ticket, which entitles you to be dropped off at most hotels within the City Centre-Kings Cross area, costs A\$3. Taxis run about A\$10. Turn a cold shoulder on the rental car agents for now: you don't need one in the city. Public transportation is excellent, and you'll save a lot of money, not to mention parking and driving hassles, if you wait to pick up a car until you leave Sydney in three days.

If you haven't yet booked your domestic flight segments, take the escalator upstairs to the departure hall and do it now. If you're wielding a "Go Australian Airpass," you'll need Ansett Flight #77 from Melbourne to Alice Springs at 10 a.m. on Day 11; Ansett NT Flight BT278 from Alice Springs to Ayers Rock at 11:35 a.m. on Day 12; Ansett Flight #285 from Alice Springs to Cairns at 10:55 a.m. on Day 16; and Ansett Flight #39 from Cairns to Brisbane at 5:15 p.m. on Day 19.

Sydney Orientation
Over 20% of all Australians live in metropolitan Sydney. These 3½ million lucky people make their homes in one of the great cities on earth. It has everything they might ask: a beautiful setting around a long, deep-blue harbor, a rich and varied cultural life, restaurants and hotels to suit all tastes and spending abilities, activities enough to support a book which could be titled "Sydney in 22 Days."

Not only is Sydney Australia's largest city; it was also its first. On January 26, 1788, Captain Arthur Phillip arrived in Port Jackson (Sydney Harbour) with his "First Fleet" of 11 ships. He landed close to the site of the modern Harbour Bridge and established a settlement in the area known today as The Rocks. Nearly three-quarters of his 1,030 passengers were convicts, most of them deported from the British Isles for petty thievery, forgery and similarly trumped-up charges. They became the foundation of the colony and the nation, and it is their success that Australia is celebrating in its Bicentennial observance in 1988.

The oldest buildings standing in Sydney today are a legacy of Governor Lachlan Macquarie (1809-1821), who set an egalitarian standard for Australia by ordering the emancipation

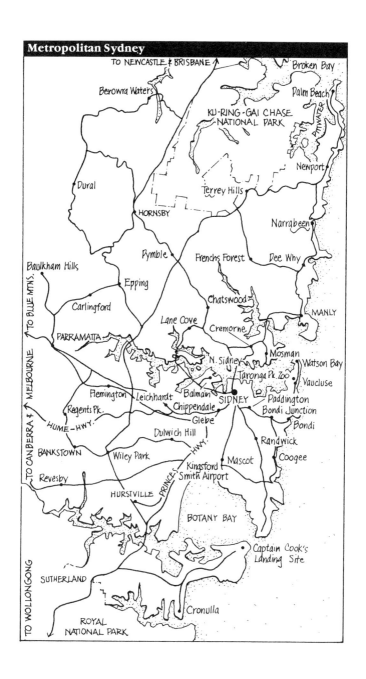

Metropolitan Sydney

of deserving convicts to give them a "fair go" alongside free settlers. Yet it wasn't until the 20th Century, first with Commonwealth status ("independence") in 1901 and later with an
influx of European immigrants, that the city really boomed.

Sydney's climate is similar to that of Los Angeles—without
the smog. The mean summer temperature (December to
February) is 78 degrees Fahrenheit; the winter mean (June to
August) is 55 degrees. Average annual rainfall is 47.5 inches,
with June the rainiest month (5.1 inches) and September the
driest (0.6 inches). With such a comfortable climate,
Sydneysiders love the outdoors. On most weekends and sunny
afternoons you'll find them on their boats in the harbour or
spangling the many fine beaches.

Though Sydney sprawls for many miles around the harbour,
it's easy to find your way around the central area. Circular Quay,
where ferries and cruise boats dock, is your point of orientation. East of the Quay, jutting into the harbour on Bennelong
Point, is the Opera House, and immediately south of it the
botanic gardens and The Domain. Macquarie Street is the main
north-south thoroughfare here. West of the Quay, George and
Pitt streets run from The Rocks (at the foot of the Harbour
Bridge) through the City Centre to Chinatown and the central
railway station. Park Street (becoming William Street) intersects
George and Pitt streets at Sydney Town Hall and proceeds east,
dissecting Hyde Park and running about a mile to Kings Cross.
The Martin Place pedestrian hall, halfway between Park Street
and Circular Quay, spans five blocks from George Street to Macquarie Street.

City Transportation
Between the subway/train, the bus and the ferry system,
Sydney is extremely well served by all forms of public transpor-
tation.

The Sydney Metropolitan Rail System (tel. 20942) serves 176
stations in nine lines running west, south, north and east of
Central Station. The City Circle subway line runs continuously
from 4:30 a.m. to midnight between Museum, St. James, Circular Quay, Wynyard, Town Hall and Central stations; the
Eastern Suburbs line connects Town Hall with Martin Place,
Kings Cross and on to Bondi Junction. System-wide maps can
be obtained from any visitor information center. Standard fares
for short distances are 60 cents.

Buses of the Urban Transit Authority of New South Wales (tel.
20543) serves every corner of the metropolis that the trains
miss. Fares start at 60 cents. A free bus service (No. 777) operates
in the central city area at 10-minute intervals from 9:30 a.m. to

3:30 p.m. Monday to Friday. Another free bus (No. 666) connects Wynyard station with the Art Gallery of New South Wales in The Domain. Tourists are well served by the Sydney Explorer, a bright red double-decker bus which runs an 18-km loop to 20 major attractions for a set fee of A$7.50. The service operates continuously from 9:30 a.m. to 5 p.m. daily at 15-minute intervals.

The Urban Transit Authority also operates the ferry service from Circular Quay (tel. 219-4735) between 6 a.m. and 11 p.m. daily. The one-way fare is A$1 west to Hunters Hill and Greenwich, or across the harbour to Mosman, Cremorne and Neutral Bay. To Manly, near the head of the harbour, it costs A$1.30 by ferry or $2.40 by hydrofoil.

Two special fares allow travelers to take advantage of all transportation systems for a reduced cost. The Day Rover, priced at A$3.80, is good for unlimited travel on train, ferry (but not hydrofoil) and bus (except the Sydney Explorer) within the Sydney area weekdays after 9 a.m., or anytime weekends. The Weekly Rover, good for seven consecutive days under similar conditions, costs A$19.

Where to Stay

Sydney's best hotels are a boomerang's throw from Circular Quay and The Rocks. The **Regent of Sydney**, 199 George St. (tel. 238-0000) is ranked among the world's elite: it's very expensive. . . but worth every penny, I'm told. Just down the street, and a small step down in price, is the **Old Sydney Parkroyal**, right in The Rocks at 55 George St. (tel. 20524).

For lower cost lodging, the best selection is in Kings Cross, Sydney's answer to London's Soho and Paris' Pigalle. There's a lot of bustle and sleaze (some call it "character") here, but no real danger as long as you mind your own business. In the moderate price backet, check out the **Melin Plaza**, a self-catering apartment hotel at 2 Springfield Ave. (tel. 356-3255). For an economy class bed, the nearby **Springfield Lodge**, 9 Springfield Ave. (tel. 358-3222), has old-world charm.

For real budget accommodation, look on Victoria Street and Hughes Street, where you'll pay as little as A$6 a night in a dorm (perhaps A$15 a night in a shared double room) at a dozen small private hotels and backpackers' hostels. There's not a lot to choose between these places; I opt for the places with TV and rec rooms, not to mention good travelers' bulletin boards. Try **The Traveler's Rest**, 156 Victoria St. (tel. 358-4606), or **The Downunder Hostel**, 25 Hughes St. (tel. 358-1143). No hostel in the Cross is a member of the International Youth Hostel Federation; there are IYH hostels further out at 262 Glebe Point Road, Glebe (tel. 692-8418); 28 Ross St., Forest

Lodge (tel. 692-0747), near Sydney University; and 407 Mar-rickville Road, Dulwich Hill (tel. 569-0272).

Where to Eat
The best restaurant strip in Sydney, both in terms of price and variety of cuisine, is Oxford Street in Darlinghurst, less than 1 km south of Kings Cross via Darlinghurst Road or Victoria Street. For less than A$10 per person, you can eat well at such diverse ethnic eateries as **Raquel's Ole Madrid** (Spanish, No. 145), **La Bella Notte** (Italian, No. 201), the **Balkan** (Greek, No. 209-215), **Momotaro** (Japanese, No. 225), **Kim** (No. 235, Vietnamese) or **Borobudur** (Indonesian, No. 263), among many others. Around the corner and down the street are Sydney's best selections for budget-watchers—**No Name** (that's what locals call it; it really doesn't have a name), 2 Chapel St., a half-block south of Stanley Street off Crown Street, and the **Metro Cafe**, 26 Burton St. west of Crown. At either, you can get simple but huge pasta-and-salad meals for around A$5. Two doors down from the Metro on Burton is the **Different Drummer**, a licensed establishment (the others are all BYO) in a lovely garden setting where steak or seafood dinners run A$6 to A$7. **Laurie's**, opposite Green Park at Victoria and Burton streets, has innovative vegetarian cuisine.

In the Cross, you'll get a square meal for a fair price at the **Bayswater Brasserie**, 32 Bayswater Road. Other moderate-priced options: **Majit's Renamed Amar's**, 69 Macleay St., for Indian curries, and **Benny's**, 12-14 Challis Ave., for Japanese and Malay cuisine.

Downtown, you can dine like an affluent tourist at the **Bennelong Restaurant** in the Opera House, or in higher style yet in the revolving restaurants atop **Sydney Tower** or **Australia Square** (which is round, incidentally). More popular among locals in a moderate price range are **Johnny Walker's Bistro** in Angel Place (near Martin Place) for steaks; the **Sorrento**, 5 Elizabeth St. (basement), for seafood; **The Old Spaghetti Factory**, 80 George St., The Rocks, for pasta and atmosphere; **Pancakes on the Rocks**, 10 Hickson Road, for 24-hour munchies; and the **Imperial Peking Harbourside**, 15 Circular Quay West, for upmarket Chinese food.

If you want to eat like the Asians, though, visit the **Chinatown Food Fair**, Dixon and Goulburn streets (third floor). Open from 11 a.m. to 11 p.m. daily (to 9 p.m. Sundays), you can sate your appetite for under A$5 while choosing your meal from over a dozen Southeast Asia-style food stalls. There's a smaller version of same at **Dixon Gourmet**, Dixon and Little Hay streets.

Away from Sydney's core, two restaurants deserve a special

mention. **Doyle's on the Beach**, at Watson's Bay near the south head of the harbour mouth, is so famous for its seafood that it runs a special shuttle ferry from a dock near Circular Quay. The **Berowra Waters Inn**, Berowra, is considered the best of all possible restaurants in Australia. To get there, you must drive an hour north from the city centre to a jetty, where you are met by a private punt. It's open Friday to Sunday only, and bookings are required.

Helpful Hints
The **Sydney Visitors Bureau** (tel. 235-2424) is in Martin Place at Elizabeth Street, smack in the middle of downtown. The office provides maps and brochures, and books seats for tours or entertainment events, 9 a.m. to 5 p.m. weekdays.

The **General Post Office** is also on Martin Place at the corner of Pitt Street. Banks are open 9:30 a.m. to 4 p.m. Monday to Thursday, 9:30 a.m. to 5 p.m. Friday. Most shops are open from 9 a.m. to 5:30 p.m. Monday to Wednesday, 9 a.m. to 9 p.m. Thursday and Friday, 9 a.m. to 12 noon Saturday.

There's a U.S. Consulate General in the T&G Building, Elizabeth and Park streets (tel. 264-7044), and a **Canadian Consulate General** on the 8th Floor of the AMP Centre, 50 Bridge St. (tel. 231-6522).

In case of emergencies, dial 000.

DAY 2
AROUND SYDNEY

Today is devoted to exploring the major sights of the city's core. Take the red double-decker bus, the Sydney Explorer (see "City Transportation," Day 1), or—better yet—walk.

Suggested Schedule	
8:00 a.m.	Breakfast at hotel.
9:00 a.m.	Take the bus, subway or walk to the Opera House, arriving for the guided tour.
10:30 a.m.	Experience the view from Sydney Tower.
11:15 a.m.	Browse through Hyde Park Barracks and The Old Mint.
12:30 p.m.	Picnic lunch in The Domain or Botanic Gardens.
1:30 p.m.	Art Gallery of N.S.W.
3:00 p.m.	Australian Museum.
4:30 p.m.	The Rocks: Start a walking tour at the visitor center, but dawdle in the shops and pubs.
7:30 p.m.	Dinner and show at the Argyle Tavern.

Sightseeing Highlights
▲▲▲**Sydney Harbour** (see Day 1)—Life in Sydney centers on the Harbour. Thirteen miles (21 km) long from its ocean heads to the mouth of the Paramatta River, with some 160 miles (250 km) of crenelled coastline, the deep blue inlet seems permanently speckled with boats of all sizes and shapes. On sunny weekend afternoons, the colorful jibs of myriad sailboats make the harbour look like a seaborne carnival. The Opera House and Harbour Bridge are its unmistakable landmarks, but there is much more to see: colonial mansions and modern architectural showcases, the skylines of downtown and North Sydney, the laughing face and looming roller coaster of Luna Park, the sandstone turrets of Fort Denison on venerable Pinchgut Island.

All Harbour cruises leave the city from Circular Quay, at the foot of Pitt Street. Ferry routes and fares are discussed in Day 1 under "City Transportation." There's also a Sydney Harbour Explorer: for a flat fee of A$12, you can spend the day shuttling between the Opera House, The Rocks, Pier 1, the Taronga Park Zoo and Watson Bay. The Explorer leaves Circular Quay daily at 10:25 and 11:55 a.m., 1:25 and 2:55 p.m. Ninety minute stopovers are permitted, with free reboarding.

There are several cruise operators. I like Captain Cook

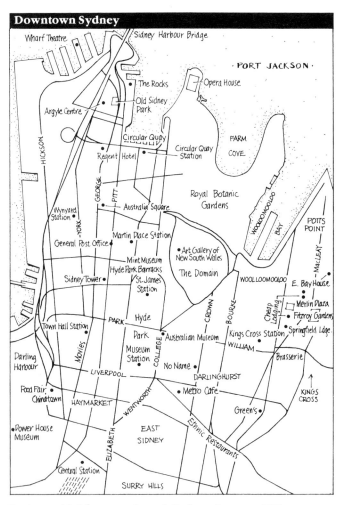

Downtown Sydney

Cruises, with 14 tour options daily from 9 a.m. to 7:30 p.m.,
varying in length from 75 minutes to six hours and in price
from $9 to $41.50. A good introductory trip is the Captain Cook
Coffee Cruise, leaving Pier 6 every day at 10 a.m. and 2 p.m. The
2½ hour trip includes refreshments.

▲▲▲**Sydney Opera House**, Bennelong Point. One of the
most unique buildings on Earth, the Opera House was designed
by Danish architect Jorn Utzon, begun in 1959 and opened in
1973. Talk about inflation: its cost was first estimated at A$7
million, but it wound up costing A$102 million! It's really much

more than a stage for operas; the complex also contains a concert hall, drama and movie theaters, a recording hall, an exhibition hall, two restaurants, six lounges, a library and archives, and various rehearsal studios, dressing rooms and administrative offices, all under the distinctive sail-like roofs.

Sixty-minute guided tours are conducted daily (except Good Friday and Christmas) from 9 a.m. to 4 p.m. Backstage tours, lasting 90 minutes, are offered Sundays only. They start from the Music Room-Exhibition foyer on the ground level; tickets are A$3.50.

A better way to appreciate the Opera House is to take in a performance. You can get a full schedule of all events at most visitor centers. The Opera House box office is open Monday to Saturday from 9 a.m. to 8:30 p.m., and Sunday from 9 a.m. to 4 p.m. You can also book by phone (with a major credit card) by calling 20525.

▲▲**Sydney Tower**—Rises 1,000 feet above the Centrepoint shopping complex off Market Street between Pitt and Castlereagh streets. Some Aussie cynics call this edifice "the bucket on the stick," but as the highest public building in the Southern Hemisphere, it's worth the trip up for the view. Open 9:30 a.m. to 9:30 p.m. Monday to Saturday, 10:30 a.m. to 4:30 p.m. Sunday and public holidays; closed Christmas. It will cost you A$3.50 to take the lift up. Lunch and dinner are served in a pair of restaurants immediately below the observation deck.

▲▲**Hyde Park Barracks**—On Queen's Square at the top of Macquarie Street. Designed by convict architect Francis Greenway (whose picture is on the A$10 bill) and erected in 1819 as a dormitory for male convicts, it has become an interesting museum of Sydney social history. Start on the top floor to learn in considerable detail about the shipment of convicts from England to Sydney, then step down to the second floor to trace the city's 19th Century development. Open 10 a.m. to 5 p.m. daily (noon to 5 p.m. Tuesday); closed Good Friday and Christmas. Free admission.

▲**The Old Mint**—Next door to the Barracks. One of Australia's oldest public buildings (1817), it was built as a hospital wing but became the first branch of the British Royal Mint outside of London after gold was discovered in 1851. Since 1982, it has been an elegant, well-organized museum of decorative art, coins and stamps. Open 10 a.m. to 5 p.m. daily (noon to 5 p.m. Wednesday); closed Good Friday and Christmas. Free admission.

▲**Art Gallery of New South Wales**—Art Gallery Road, The Domain. Sydney's (but not Australia's) best art museum, it is interesting for its survey of Aussie paintings through the 19th and 20th centuries. A major 1987-88 expansion will add a sculpture

terrace, Asian art gallery and several theaters. Open 10 a.m. to 5
p.m. daily (noon to 5 p.m. Sunday); closed Good Friday and
Christmas. Free admission.

▲**Royal Botanic Gardens**—The second botanic gardens in
the Southern Hemisphere are a pleasant place for a stroll or a
picnic. Open 8 a.m. to sunset daily. Free guided walks are conducted at 9:30 a.m. Wednesday and 10 a.m. Friday from the
visitor center.

▲▲**The Australian Museum**—Corner William and College
streets (opposite Hyde Park). This museum is of special interest
for superb exhibits of Aboriginal and Papua New Guinean
lifestyles. It also has good displays of Australian geological and
natural history. In 1988, a Pacific art gallery and other new exhibits are scheduled to open. Open 10 a.m. to 5 p.m. daily
(noon to 5 p.m. Monday); closed Good Friday and Christmas.
Free admission.

▲▲**Powerhouse Museum**—Harris and Mary Ann streets,
Ultimo. A highly acclaimed new science and technology
museum scheduled to open for the Bicentennial in 1988, this
will feature everything from steam engines to the space race
to the history of the brewing industry in New South Wales.
Many displays are hands-on. An advance exhibition was open
to the public in 1987. Open 10 a.m. to 5 p.m. daily.

▲▲**Darling Harbour**—This urban reclamation project on the
west end of downtown Sydney will be "the place to go" when
it opens in 1988. In addition to a hotel/casino and convention
center, it will include eight waterfront restaurants and cafes, 100
retail shops, night clubs, a maritime museum and aquarium, a
Chinese garden and a waterfront promenade. A monorail will
connect Darling Harbour to the city center.

▲**Elizabeth Bay House**—Onslow Avenue, Elizabeth Bay.
Close to King's Cross but on the Sydney Explorer bus route, this
elegant 1835 colonial mansion has been fully restored to period
decor. Open 10 a.m. to 4:30 p.m. Tuesday through Sunday.
Adult admission $2.50; Sydney Explorer patrons $2.

▲▲▲**The Rocks**—Sydney's most historic district is located
just northwest of Circular Quay. The oldest building still standing, Cadmans Cottage, was built in 1816, but most structures
date from the 1840s to 1880s, during which time this was
Sydney's main commercial and maritime quarter.

To see the area properly, you should guide yourself on a walking tour beginning from The Rocks Visitor Centre, 104 George
St.—open Monday to Friday 8:30 a.m. to 4:30 p.m., weekends
and holidays 10 a.m. to 5 p.m. You can pick up a map describing
various sites, but the best way to explore is simply to amble and
browse, ducking into the various small shops, art galleries,
museums and pubs. Several pubs, including The Old Push,

Phillips Foote and the venerable Hero of Waterloo, feature live "trad jazz" performances during after-work "happy hour" and on weekends.

The highlight of The Rocks is the **Argyle Centre**, a four-story complex of various artisans' galleries, antique shops and cafes. Housed in a group of 1828 sandstone bond stores and warehouses, it authentically preserves the atmosphere of the period—and nowhere better than the **Argyle Tavern**, a great spot for an Australian night out. As you fill up on Sydney rock oysters, grilled barramundi or steak-and-kidney pie, the Jolly Swagman Show will introduce you to a variety of Aussie bush ballads and folk songs, the Aboriginal didgeridoo (a primitive droning instrument) and the fine art of shearing a sheep. . . right on stage. Showtime is 8 to 9:30 nightly; come by 7:30 to place your order and beat the rush. A warning: shoe-string travelers may want to think twice before purging their wallets of A$42.50 (per person) for the dinner and show.

DAY 3
MORE OF SYDNEY

I'd spend today touring the Eastern Suburbs, but there are many other options—take the ferry to Manly and the zoo, for instance, or travel to the Blue Mountains or the Hunter Valley.

Suggested Schedule	
9:00 a.m.	Take the subway (Blue Line) to Bondi Junction, then catch Bus No. 380 or 389 to Bondi Beach. You'll arrive by 9:30 a.m., giving you two hours to soak in rays and surf culture before lunch.
11:30 a.m.	Catch a city bus north up the coast to Watson's Bay for a seafood lunch at Doyle's.
1:30 p.m.	Bus No. 325 heads back toward the city. Stop off at Vaucluse House, an 1830s mansion.
2:30 p.m.	Disembark in Double Bay for a look at Sydney's version of Rodeo Drive.
3:30 p.m.	Have a cab drop you in Paddington at the New Edition Bookshop, 328 Oxford St., where you can obtain free "The Paddington Book" with a map and suggested walking tour.
5:30 p.m.	Continue to the Cross by foot, bus or taxi. It's your night to paint the town red.

Sightseeing Highlights
▲▲**Bondi** (pronounced Bond-eye)—It is the most famous of all Sydney's beaches. It's not the most attractive, unless perhaps you're talking about the topless south end of the beach; but there seems to be more tradition and a livelier crowd here than at other Eastern Suburbs beaches, especially during summer when surf lifesaving contests are held throughout Australia.
▲**Vaucluse House**—Olala Avenue, Vaucluse, was built in 1803 and became the home of William Charles Wentworth, the Thomas Jefferson of Australia, from 1827 to 1853. A beachfront manor which sits in 27 acres of park and garden, it has been lavishly refurbished in the style of Wentworth's time. Open 10 a.m. to 4:30 p.m. Tuesday to Sunday. Adult admission is $2.50.
▲**Double Bay**—May be Australia's most fashionable few blocks. Knox Street, Cross Street and New South Head Road are lined with designer boutiques, exclusive jewelers and antique shops. You'll see Sydney's beautiful people sizing each other up at sidewalk cafes and delis.

▲▲**Paddington**—May be downmarket from Double Bay, but it's upmarket from most of the rest of Sydney. Known locally as "Paddo," this hilly neighborhood might strike Washingtonians as being a little like Georgetown. Here, the young, upwardly mobile population has put its restoration energies into Victorian terrace houses rather than brownstone manors. Many artists, musicians and educators live among the trendy arts and crafts galleries and numerous fine restaurants and pubs.

Special attractions in Paddington include an open-air market called the **Village Bazaar**, held from 9 a.m. to 4 p.m. every Saturday at the corner of Newcombe and Oxford Street, and the **Victoria Barracks**, a superb example of British colonial military architecture on Oxford Street opposite Hopewell Street. If you're here on Tuesday, see the impressive changing of the guard at 11 a.m.

▲**Manly**—Is a good destination for those who prefer to spend time on the water instead of in trains and buses. Spread across a narrow neck of land separating the Harbour from the Tasman Sea, it has a quaint pedestrian mall connecting the famed surfing beach with a still-water swimming area. Manly's attractions include a Marineland (open 10 a.m. to 5 p.m. daily), an amusement pier, a series of waterslides, and an art gallery/museum. Manly is easily reached from Circular Quay by ferry (A$1.30 each way) or hydrofoil (A$2.40 each way).

▲**Taronga Park Zoo**—Bradleys Head Road, Mosman, is an excellent place to get an introduction to Australia's unique wildlife. Its exhibits include a treetop koala exhibit, a platypus house, a rainforest aviary and a special nocturnal house. You can travel there either by ferry from Circular Quay (A$1 each way) or by Bus NO. 237 or 238 across the Sydney Harbour Bridge. Open daily year-round, 9 a.m. to 5 p.m. Admission is $5.

Birkenhead Point—A shopping center off Victoria Road in the harborside suburb of Drummoyne, a few miles west of the city center, might be considered a rainy-day option. There are some 130 shops and restaurants, plus the **Lego Centre**, one of only two permanent exhibitions in the world of models built from these childhood building blocks. Open daily 9:15 a.m. to 5:15 p.m., Thursdays until 9 p.m.

The **Sydney Maritime Museum**, with a fleet of historic ships, is also located here. It's open Monday 1:30 to 5 p.m., Tuesday to Friday 10 a.m. to 5 p.m., Saturday and Sunday 11:30 a.m. to 4:30 p.m. Birkenhead Point is reach by bus No. 500 or 502 from Circular Quay to the Iron Cove Bridge.

Day Trips from Sydney
If you're inclined to rent your car a day early, here are some
worthwhile day trip options.
▲**The Blue Mountains**—Once a forboding natural barrier to
early settlers, are now a favorite weekend getaway for
Sydneysiders. Their undeclared capital is Katoomba, a small
town 106 km (66 miles) west of Sydney, though they spread
from Penrith to Lithgow. The mountains' most famous attraction is **The Three Sisters**, an unusual rock formation
associated with Aboriginal legend. A cablecar and scenic
railway at the site make it a honeymooners' delight. There are
also spectacular caves and waterfalls, art galleries and historic
museums.
▲**Pittwater and Broken Bay**—At the mouth of the Hawkesbury
River marking the northern boundary of the Sydney
metropolis, are places of great natural beauty. They're best seen
from the deck of a private yacht, but they can also be
thoroughly appreciated from the land. Drive north up Sydney's
east coast through Mona Vale to **Palm Beach**, or better yet,
spend an afternoon bushwalking in **Ku-ring-gai Chase National Park**.
▲**Old Sydney Town**—Near Gosford about 70 km (43 miles)
north of downtown Sydney, recreates the Sydney Cove settlement as it is thought to have been in the early 19th Century.
Only authentic materials and methods were used in building the
50-acre theme park. Soldiers, convicts and free settlers, all in
period costume, continually act out scenes from the colony's
history. Open 10 a.m. to 5 p.m. Wednesday to Sunday; daily
during school holidays. Admission is $8.50. A rail tour, leaving
Sydney's Central Station at 9:15 a.m. and returning shortly after
6:30 p.m., costs $20 for adults and includes admission.
▲**The Hunter Valley**—Near Cessnock some 180 km (110
miles) north of Sydney, is Australia's oldest wine-producing
district and its second most important (after the Barossa Valley
near Adelaide). The 34 wineries here are best known for their
soft reds. Most are open for tasting daily from 9 or 10 a.m. to
about 5 p.m. Hungerford Hill, Rothbury Estate, Tyrrells and
Wyndham Estate are among the most highly regarded.

Night Life
Anything and everything goes in **Kings Cross**, several
meandering blocks of burlesque shows, theater restaurants,
discotheques, tattoo parlors and streetwalkers where Darlinghurst Road, Victoria Street, Bayswater Road and William
Street come together a mile east of the city center. Some call the
Cross "bohemian," others "sleazy"; the truth may lie somewhere
between. People-watching is the best form of entertainment

here; grab a window table and a cup of capuccino at an open-air cafe. You might also get a kick out of the automated Ray Charles double playing piano and singing at **Jo Jo Ivory's** in the Potts Point Sheraton, 40 Macleay St.

To find out what's happening on any given day in the greater Sydney area, get hold of *The Sydney Morning Herald's* Friday "Metro" section, with listings of the entertainment week ahead. Musical offerings are broken down into classical, jazz, country, folk, acoustic and rock, with the latter category as large as the other five combined. Paddington (try the **Grand National Hotel** or the **Windsor Castle Hotel**) and Bondi (the **Royal Hotel** is best) have especially large concentrations of music pubs, but you'll find them everywhere.

The best modern jazz in Sydney is consistently found at **The Basement**, 29 Reiby Place near Circular Quay.

If you're strictly into meeting people without having to shout over the din of music, check out some of the city's wine bars— like **French's** on Oxford Street in Darlinghurst, **Soren's** in Woolloomooloo or **The Stoned Crow** in Crow's Nest, across the Harbour Bridge. In North Sydney you'll also find **Sheila's**, a singles bar with provocative coasters that read: "If you're look-ing for a friend, leave this side up."

Live theater is extremely popular in Sydney. Aside from the Opera House, you can take in fine productions at **The Theatre Royal** on King Street, **The Wharf Theatre** on Pier 4 (near The Rocks), the **Nimrod Theatre** in Chippendale and others.

Lower George Street has the greatest concentration of cinema houses for moviegoers. All major-studio American films are shown here, but don't miss an opportunity to see some of the outstanding movies made in Australia today.

An Australian phenomenon is the Leagues Club, of which rugby league clubs and returned servicemen's league clubs are most prevalent. Depending upon their size, they usually include a small gambling casino (with slot machines), a restaurant and bar, and an entertainment lounge, often with live music on weekends. This is where the working man typically takes his wife or girlfriend for a night out. While they are memberships clubs, overseas visitors are normally welcome. Two of the big-gest are the **South Sydney Junior Rugby League Club**, 556 Anzac Parade, Kingsford, and the **St. George Leagues Club**, 124 Princes Highway, Kogarah.

DAY 4
SYDNEY TO CANBERRA

Leave Australia's queen city and drive south to Canberra, the national capital, pausing en route at historic Gledswood homestead and Berrima. In Canberra, take time for an overview of the foundation and continuing evolution of this attractive, specially created city.

Suggested Schedule

8:00 a.m.	Pick up your reserved rental car and head out of Sydney via the Hume Highway.
9:30 a.m.	Arrive at Gledswood Homestead and wander through the working colonial farm.
10:45 a.m.	Leave for Berrima.
11:30 a.m.	Explore Berrima, a sandstone-and-brick village appearing very much today as it did in 1831. Lunch at the Surveyor General Inn, the oldest continuously licensed pub in Australia.
1:30 p.m.	Leave for Canberra.
3:30 p.m.	On arrival, drive straight to the Regatta Point Planning Exhibition on Lake Burley Griffin. Study the models and see the video to understand the grand plan for this 20th Century capital.
4:30 p.m.	Capture the view from the top of Mount Ainslie.
5:00 p.m.	Move into your accommodation. Plan on a quiet evening; most of them are just that in Canberra.

Leaving Sydney
When you obtain your rental car, double-check to be certain your agent has provided you with a Gregory's or UBD street guide to Sydney. That's your passport out of the metropolis in case you get lost.

Most visitors get their car at a rental agent on William Street, between Kings Cross and downtown. Proceed west through Hyde Park, turn left on Pitt Street and follow the signs to Liverpool. The Hume Highway, Route 31, branches south (to the left) off the Great Western Highway near Summer Hill, 8 km from William Street.

The Hume Highway
Soon after leaving Liverpool, about 30 km from the Hume Highway junction, the highway becomes a four-lane freeway. It

stays that way (with only a couple of slowdowns) all the way to
Canberra—in fact, to Melbourne—enabling you to drive the
294 km (183 miles) from Sydney to the capital in 3 ½ hours, if
you so chose.

Our tour route, however, involves a few diversions. At the
point where the freeway begins, turn right on Route 89,
Camden Valley Way (the old Hume Highway), to the community
of Catherine Field. It's about 10 km further to the historic
Gledswood Homestead, built in 1810 by convict labor and
now classified by the National Trust and the Heritage Commission. Guided tours of the homestead, winery (in a former coach
house) and working farm are offered daily from 9 a.m. to 5 p.m.
Sheep shearing, boomerang throwing and other demonstrations are often presented.

▲▲**Berrima** has recently been bypassed by the new freeway,
making its colonial isolation all the more appealing. Situated
128 km (80 miles) from Sydney and 166 km (103 miles) from
Canberra, this village (founded in 1831) is a historical gem. Pick
up a walking tour map at the Georgian-style **courthouse**,
where the first jury trial in the New South Wales colony was
held in 1843. (It's open 10 a.m. to 4 p.m. daily; admission is 60
cents.) The **jail**, built in 1839, closed in 1902 but reopened in
1949 after extensive reconstruction (and still in use), was one of
the most feared in Australia in the mid-19th Century.

About two dozen government buildings, early churches and
private manors have survived the passage of time. Many of them
may contain galleries, antique and crafts shops, restaurants and
cafes serving Devonshire teas. At the **Surveyor General Inn**,
which celebrates its 154th anniversary in business in 1988, you
can cook your own steak lunch, pile it high with a salad bar and
potatoes, and wash it down with a beer for under A$10.

A further diversion off the Hume Highway from Berrima
would lead you through the charming village of **Bundanoon** at
the edge of Lush Morton National Park. Time's a-wastin', however. Return to the freeway, drive right on through the big farming center of Goulburn (pop. 25,000), waving at the campy
"world's largest Merino sheep" sculpture as you pass. Twelve
km further on, bear left onto the Federal Highway and slide by
the rim of large (but usually dry) Lake George into the
Australian Capital Territory.

Canberra Orientation
Visitors often find Canberra like a tree without roots, a building
without a foundation. Indeed, the city is too young to have
developed much heritage of its own. Like Washington, D.C.,
Canberra, A.C.T., is strictly a government town—but its
250,000 people haven't had a 187-year history to develop a feel-

ing of heritage. It wasn't until 1901 that Melbourne and Sydney, throwing up their political arms in frustration over persistent squabbling for the right to be the national capital, finally compromised and agreed to construct a new city between the two metropolises.

In 1912, an American architect named Walter Burley Griffin won an international contest to design the capital. Following his plans, 2,366 square km (913 square miles) of sheep-grazing land was transformed into the Australian Capital Territory, and within that plot, the new city of Canberra was built. (The name "Canberra" was derived from an Aboriginal term meaning "meeting place.") In 1927, all government functions were moved here from Melbourne.

Burley Griffin's grandiose plan has taken far longer to complete than anyone imagined. Between two world wars, a Great Depression and much political in-fighting, construction funds have been hard to come by. At this writing, in fact, Canberra is still not completed to the architect's specifications! After 60 years of legislative debates in a provisional parliament house, a magnificent new Parliament House should be finished just in time for the Australian Bicentennial in 1988.

Canberra's design carefully balances natural features—low, bush-cloaked mountains and lovely, meandering Lake Burley Griffin—with geometrical patterns, mainly a series of concentric circles interconnected by strong lines. Capital Hill, site of the new Parliament, and City Hill, around which most commercial functions revolve, are 3 km apart, linked across the deep blue lake by Commonwealth Avenue. Each "hill" is the hub of a series of streets which spread from the center like the spokes of a wheel.

Northbourne Avenue, on which you'll arrive from the north, runs straight as an arrow for over 4 km directly to City Hill. Soon after you circumnavigate the hill, but before crossing the lake, look for directional signs to the **Canberra Planning Exhibition** on Regatta Point, operated by the National Capital Development Commission. Put preconceived notions aside; if you have any interest in the creative process, it isn't boring. In effect it's a historical museum, describing the text, photograph and audiovisual presentation the creation of Canberra from virtually uninhabited bush. A huge three-dimensional model of the city helps you locate points of interest. Open 9 a.m. to 5 p.m. daily (except Christmas); admission is free. A snack bar and souvenir shop are on a terrace overlooking the lake.

Of several hills with lookouts over the city, the best—from the standpoint of understanding Canberra's layout—is **Mount Ainslie** in the northeast quadrant. Not only is it the highest at 842 meters (2,772 feet); from the top, you can look straight down across the stalwart Australian War Memorial to Anzac

Parade, which neatly bisects the Federal Triangle and affords a direct view of the provisional and new Parliament Houses.

The highest viewpoint in Canberra is actually atop the striking 195-meter (640-foot) Telecom Tower on **Black Mountain** west of City Hill. But unless you dine in the revolving restaurant, you'll have to pay to gain access to the three public viewing galleries. Another lookout is on **Red Hill**, south of Capital Hill, with a restaurant offering panoramic views of the southern suburbs.

Canberra's climate, quite logically, is unlike that of any of the seaside state capitals. Located about 120 km (75 miles) inland and at 580 metres (1,900 feet) elevation in a spur of the Great Dividing Range, its summers are hotter and drier than other major cities and its winters colder, with occasional (if rare) snow flurries.

City Transportation
If you arrive in Canberra without a car at the airport, railway depot or bus station, you're not stranded. The ACTION public bus network runs through the city and its suburbs from 6 a.m. to 11:30 p.m. daily (8:30 a.m. to 6:30 p.m. Sunday), with fares of 60 cents to most destinations. No. 230 operates to Regatta Point and along the north shore of Lake Burley Griffin; No. 302 runs from the city to the Australian War Memorial; No. 357 connects City Hill with the rail station via the National Library and provisional Parliament House; No. 380 plies the 8 km (five miles) between the youth hostel and downtown.

Better designed for the tourist is the **Canberra Explorer**. This unmistakable bright red bus runs its narrated 25-km (15½-mile) circuit seven times every day from 9:40 a.m. to 4:35 p.m., making scheduled stops at major attractions and hotels. You can buy a day ticket for $7, allowing you to disembark anywhere and reboard an hour or two later, or pay $2.50 for a one-hour tour.

Where to Stay
The greatest concentration of accommodations in all price categories is along Northbourne Avenue, the main thoroughfare entering Canberra from the north. Regarded by some as the best is the **Canberra International**, 242 Northbourne Ave., Dickson, ACT 2602 (tel. 47-6966), with luxury rooms and a garden atmosphere. I'm happy in the moderate price range at **Down Town Spero's Motel**, 82 Northbourne Ave., Canberra, ACT 2601 (tel. 49-1388), an easy three-block stroll from the commercial center around City Hill.

You'll find adequate economy-class lodging at **Tall Trees Lodge**, Stephen and Sherbrooke Streets, Ainslie, ACT 2602 (tel. 47-9200). The **Gowrie Private Hotel**, 210 Northbourne Ave.,

Braddon, ACT 2602 (tel. 49-6033), has twin 10-story towers
containing 569 simple rooms and a big round floor cafeteria.
   True budget accommodation is hard to come by in Canberra,
but the **National Memorial Youth Hostel** is on Dryandra
Street in O'Connor, ACT 2601 (tel. 48-9759).

Where to Eat
The most central area for dining is Garema Place, a spacious
pedestrian mall east of Northbourne Avenue and north of London Circuit, just above City Hill. There's a wide range of
choices here, from candlelit meals to fast-food takeaway.
Dorette's Bistro, upstairs at 17 Garema Place (near Bunda
Street), is one of my favorites; it's a self-styled Bohemian cafe
with live classical and jazz music on alternate nights. **Mama's
Trattoria**, 7 Garema Place, offers big pasta meals for no more
than A$7. A couple of blocks away is the 24-hour **Lovely Lady
Pancake Parlour**, East Row and Alinga Street, with full meals
A$5-$7 and a bottomless coffee cup. Not far away, near City Hill
on Northbourne Avenue, **Boyd's Cafe** at No. 47 and the
Private Bin at No. 50 offer bistro menus and entertainment.
Vegetarians congregate at the **Honeydew Wholemeal**, 55 North-
bourne Ave.
   Downtown, upscale favorites among politicians and local
businessmen are the **Fringe Benefits** brasserie, 54 Marcus
Clarke St., and **Seasons**, in the Canberra Theatre Center, both
serving continental cuisine.
   Not far from Garema Place, on Lonsdale Street, **The Eureka
Stockade** at No. 17 is a local favorite for steaks and beer. Op-
posite at No. 14-16 are the **Siamese Kitchen**, with spicy
Southeast Asian cuisine for $8 to $10, and the **Tipsy Gypsy**, a
Hungarian restaurant. Other ethnic restaurants in the Civic Cen-
tre area include Chinese, Indian, Vietnamese and Lebanese.
   Worthy of special note are **Tilley Devine's Cafe Gallery**, 96
Wattle St., Lynehan, a feminist-operated establishment which
doesn't admit men unless accompanied by women; the **Tau**, on
Mort Street directly behind Spero's, a vegetarian and Middle
Eastern restaurant operated by a community theater group; the
Canberra Tradesmen's Union Club, Badham Street, Dickson,
with reasonably priced bistro meals served in restored trams;
and a pair of cafeterias in Australian National University's stud-
ent center, the **ANU Refectory** and the **Asian Bistro**.

Helpful Hints
The **Canberra Tourist Bureau** (tel. 45-6405 or 45-6464) has
its main offices in the Jolimont Centre on Northbourne Avenue
near London Circuit. It's open weekdays 8:30 a.m. to 5:15 p.m.
and Saturdays 9 to 11:30 a.m. More convenient for those driving

into town from the north is the **Visitor Information Centre**, on Northbourne Avenue just south of the junctions of the Federal and Barton highways, open daily (except Christmas) from 9 a.m. to 5 p.m.

The **General Post Office** adjoins the Jolimont Centre at Alinga and Moore streets. Banks open from 9:30 a.m. to 4 p.m. Monday to Thursday, an hour later on Friday. Shops are generally open 9 a.m. to 5:30 p.m. Monday to Friday, 9 a.m. to 4 p.m. Saturday. (Some stay open later Friday nights but close by noon Saturday.)

The elegant **U.S. Embassy** is at State Circle and Perth Avenue in Yarralumla, near Capital Hill (tel. 73-3711). The **Canadian Embassy** is on Commonwealth Avenue (tel. 73-3844).

In case of emergencies, dial 000.

DAY 5
CANBERRA

Explore the national capital. Start at the new Parliament House;
if the Senate and House of Representatives are in session, you
can view the proceedings from a public gallery. (If you're here
before May 1988, see the model of the new House at the exhibition hall, then attend session at the provisional house.) Take a
drive through the Yarralumla area to see the impressive row of
national embassies, then lunch at the High Court, inspect the
National Gallery and visit the Australian War Memorial
museum.

Suggested Schedule

9:00 a.m.	View Australia's new Parliament House or preview it from the Exhibition Centre.
9:30 a.m.	Get in line for a 10:00 a.m. session of the Senate or House of Representatives at the provisional (or new) Parliament House.
11:00 a.m.	Drive through Canberra's "Embassy Row."
12:00 noon	Visit the High Court and have lunch in its cafe.
1:30 p.m.	Peruse the Australian National Gallery.
3:00 p.m.	Spend a couple hours at the Australian War Memorial Museum.
5:00 p.m.	Hire a canoe for a trip on Lake Burley Griffin or return to your hotel and relax.
7:00 p.m.	Dine in Garema Place.

Sightseeing Highlights
▲▲▲The New Parliament House—With its unmistakable $4
million flagpole, will officially open on May 9, 1988. Until then,
visitors must stop in at the Exhibition Centre on State Circle
near Canberra Avenue, where a scale model of the new Parliament
House, an audiovisual program, and numerous photographs
and architectural drawings are displayed. (Open 9 a.m. to 6 p.m.
daily except Christmas and Good Friday.) The designers—the
American firm of Mitchell/Giurgola and Australian architect
Richard Thorp—kept intact Walter Burley Griffin's original plan
for Canberra with gently curving walls and careful landscaping
picking up the axis pattern of earlier roads and buildings. The
266-foot, four-legged flagpole will become the emblem of
Australian government. Excavation of the site began in 1981; as
of spring 1987, construction was going ahead of schedule. The
final cost is estimated at over A$1 billion.

▲▲▲**The Provisional Parliament House**—Soon to surrender its legislative badge, has been the seat of Australia's federal government since 1927. A graceful white building in a park-like setting on King George Terrace, it will host the Senate and House of Representatives for the final time in early 1988.

Parliament is in session from March to November. Business is conducted in the traditional "Westminster" fashion, complete with powdered wigs. Sessions commence at 2 and 8 p.m. Monday and Tuesday, 10 a.m. and 2 p.m. Wednesday, 10 a.m. and 8 p.m. Thursday, and at 9 a.m. (Senate) or 10 a.m. (House) and again at 2 p.m. on Friday. There's no admission, but you may need advance bookings to see the House of Representatives (call 72-1211 or 72-6606 on arrival in Canberra). Arrive a little early to get in line. You'll be admitted on a first-come, first-serve basis, and allowed to stay and watch for 25 minutes.

Even if you don't manage to catch Parliament in session, come to see where proceedings take place and look at the gallery of oil portraits of Queen Elizabeth II and past governor-generals and parliamentarians. Visitors are admitted through a ground floor security entrance Monday to Saturday from 9 a.m. to 5 p.m. and Sunday from 9:30 a.m. to 5 p.m.

▲▲**The High Court of Australia**—In an impressive concrete-and-glass structure on the shore of Lake Burley Griffin, is the nation's ultimate court of appeal. The Great Hall—the main public area—has two huge murals depicting the justice system and the states. Ramps connect it with courtrooms on three succeeding floors, decorated with indigenous woodwork, woven tapestries, sculptures and other native artworks. When in session, the court sits from 10:15 a.m. to 12:45 p.m. and 2:15 to 4:15 p.m. weekdays. The building is open to visitors 9:45 a.m. to 4:30 p.m. most days. A licensed cafe, overlooking Lake Burley Griffin, serves excellent light meals for A$5 or less.

▲▲**The Australian National Gallery**—Connected by a first-floor walkway to the High Court building, has a fine if limited collection of Australian and foreign paintings, sculpture and decorative arts. Free guided tours of the Australian art section are offered daily at 11:15 a.m. and 2:15 p.m. The gallery is open 10 a.m. to 5 p.m. daily except Good Friday and Christmas; admission is $2.

▲**The National Library of Australia**—West of the High Court on the lakefront, has an Australian art collection of its own, displayed daily from 9 a.m. to 4:45 p.m. in the Rex Nan Kivell Room. Some 3.6 million volumes of books are stored in 10 acres of space and on 47 miles of shelves. The main reading room is open to the public 9:30 a.m. to 10 p.m. Monday to Thursday, 9:30 a.m. to 4:45 p.m. Friday and Saturday, and 1:30 to 4:45 p.m. Sunday.

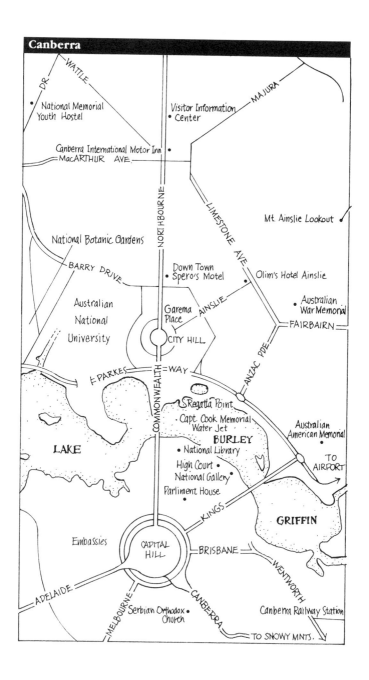

▲▲▲**The Australian War Memorial**—Is the country's best museum of any kind. Whether you view war as glorious, horrible or a bit of both, this somber memorial will make a definite impression. Inscribed with the names of more than 102,000 Australians who died in service to their country, it stares straight down tree-lined Anzac Parade and across Lake Burley Griffin at Parliament House, 4 km (2 ½ miles) distant. Built in the 1930s and expanded often since, the museum/art gallery traces Aussie military history from British colonial times through the First World War tragedy of Gallipoli and the Second World War attacks on Darwin to Australia's more modern involvement in the Vietnam conflict. Free guided tours are available weekdays at 10:30 a.m. and 1:30 p.m. Open daily 9 a.m. to 4:45 p.m. Free admission.

▲**Lake Burley Griffin**—The vivid blue centerpiece of Canberra, is highlighted by the Captain Cook Memorial Water Jet (sending a column of water 430 feet above the lake from 10 a.m. to noon and again 2 to 4 p.m. daily) and the Carillon (a 53-bell tower with free recitals on Wednesdays, Sundays and holidays). You can cruise the lake for an hour or two aboard the "City of Canberra" or "Lady Claire" (leaving at noon and 1 p.m. daily, cost A$6 to $9), or rent a rowboat, canoe, paddleboat or windsurfer (A$7 to $10 an hour). All water activities are centered on West Basin in Acton Park.

Nightlife
Canberra's evening activity is pretty tame. **Juliana's**, in Noah's Lakeside International Hotel on London Circuit, is the top discotheque; **Dorette's Bistro** is good for light classical and jazz. Things liven up a bit on Friday and Saturday night, when several small bars and taverns feature live entertainment for dancing. Most residents find their diversions at RSL, leagues or other clubs in Canberra or neighboring Queanbeyan, N.S.W. Visitors are welcome; check out the **Canberra Labor Club**, Chandler Street in Belconnen; the **Canberra Workers Club**, University Avenue and Children's Street, City; or the **Royals Rugby Union Football Club**, Weston Creek.

The modern **Canberra Theatre Centre in Civic Square**, off London Circuit, contains a theater, playhouse, gallery, restaurant and rehearsal room. Everything from serious drama to world-class ballet to Gilbert and Sullivan to rock concerts is presented here. Call the box office (tel. 57-1077) for current offerings and prices.

DAY 6
CANBERRA TO BEECHWORTH

Today's route leads past the alpine resort of Thredbo in the Snowy Mountains; via Corryons, reputed home of poet Banjo Paterson's "Man from Snowy River"; to Beechworth, a town straight out of the 19th Century gold-rush era.

Suggested Schedule

8:30 a.m.	Leave Canberra, driving via Cooma to Thredbo.
11:30 a.m.	Arrive at Thredbo. Take an hour for lunch and a look around, or buy some sandwich makings and stop for a picnic further down the road.
2:30 p.m.	After a drive down the Alpine Way through the Snowy Mountains, visit tiny Corryong to see the Man from Snowy River Folk Museum.
4:30 p.m.	Arrive in Yackandandah, for a short tour of this village classified by the National Trust.
5:30 p.m.	Reach the fascinating town of Beechworth, whose main street has changed little in 100 years.

Today's Drive
Follow the signs off Canberra Avenue, southeast of Capital Hill, to reach the Monaro Highway. **Cooma**, 117 km (73 miles) south of Canberra, is about a 1½ hour drive. Often considered the "gateway" to the Snowy Mountains because most skiers pass through it en route to the various resorts, this town of 8,000 also is headquarters of the Snowy Mountains Hydro-Electric Scheme, a massive project which created dams, power stations and high-altitude lakes throughout the range west of here.

Thredbo, another 96 km (53 miles) of winding road west across the Snowy River, is built like a Tyrolean village with chalets dotting its alpine slopes. Regarded as Australia's No. 1 ski resort, it is also a popular summer escape with the country's highest golf course (1370m or 4,495 feet), tennis courts and horse riding trails. Looming above the snowfields at the top of its Crackenback chairlift is Australia's highest peak, Mount Kosciusko, 2229m (7,313 feet) in elevation. It's an easy walk for summer day-hikers and winter "langlaufers," cross-country skiers. Non-skiers find spring the best time to visit, when the slopes are covered with wildflowers. Twenty separate lodges and a youth hostel provide beds and/or meals for skiers and other vacationers. The Thredbo Alpine Hotel, at the foot of the mountain, is a good choice for lunch with a view.

Alpine Way runs for 74 km (46 miles) through Kosciusko National Park from Thredbo to Khancoban. More than half of the route is gravel, but it's well-graded and is not normally (snow or heavy rain excepted) a difficult or dangerous drive. On the other hand, it's tremendously scenic, offering numerous vistas of the dense bush surrounding the headwaters of the Murray River, Australia's longest. On the off-chance you've thrown a fishing pole in with your gear, the streams and lakes along this this road are a good place to cast a line. Buy a license as you pass through Cooma (A$5 for 30 days).

Upon reaching **Khancoban**, a tiny township established for hydro-electric workers, you will have dropped nearly 3,500 feet from Thredbo. Follow the signs across the Murray River into the state of Victoria. It's 21 km (13 miles) to **Corryong**.

A broad main street establishes the character of this country center. If you didn't see the movie starring Kirk Douglas and several Australian actors, be sure to read Banjo Paterson's short but stirring ballad, "The Man from Snowy River," before you arrive. Jack Riley, generally regarded as the model for the poem, made his home in Corryong and is buried in the town cemetery. He and his legend are remembered at the **Man from Snowy River Folk Museum** with an eclectic but charming variety of exhibits including skis used by 19th Century gold miners. Located at the west end of town, it's open only from 2 to 3 p.m. Monday to Saturday. Admission is $2.

Rather than backtracking on the Murray Valley Highway, proceed directly west about 120 km (75 miles) via Tallangatta to **Yackandandah**. (You can avoid the bottleneck of the Albury-Wodonga area by cutting over to the Kiewa Valley Highway near Tangambalanga). So important is Yackandandah, historically and architecturally, that the entire township and surrounding hills are classified by the National Trust. Why the hills? Because the creeks and 19th Century gold diggings still yield alluvial gold to amateur prospectors. Take a few minutes to stroll the tree-lined avenues of town and photograph the buildings.

Beechworth

The most historically interesting town in northeast Victoria is **Beechworth**, 24 km (15 miles) southwest of Yackandandah. Established in 1839, it soon became one of Australia's richest goldfields, yielding 4.1 million ounces between 1852 and 1862. Commercial mining continued until 1920, and weekend panners still find gold in the creeks today.

By the time you arrive, the visitor information center in The Rock Cavern, at Ford and Camp streets, will probably be closed. You can take a "formal" self-guided tour tomorrow morning. For now, check into an accommodation with appropriate 19th

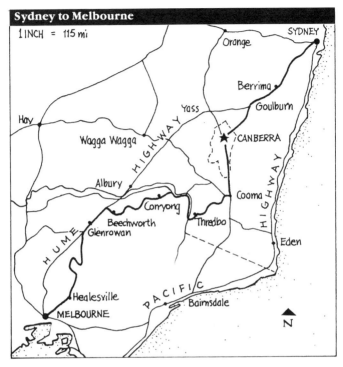

Sydney to Melbourne

1 INCH = 115 mi

SYDNEY

Orange

Berrima

Goulburn

Yass

Hay

Wagga Wagga

HIGHWAY

CANBERRA

HIGHWAY

Albury

Cooma

Corryong

Beechworth

Thredbo

Glenrowan

HUME

Eden

Healesville

PACIFIC

Bairnsdale

MELBOURNE

N

Century atmosphere, dine and get some shuteye.

Rose Cottage Bed and Breakfast, 42 Camp St. (tel. 057/
28-1069), is a quaint four-bedroom home fully furnished with
Victorian antiques. The price of A$36 single, A$49 double includes a full breakfast. Next door, the more commonplace but
comfortable **Carriage Motor Inn**, 44 Camp St. (tel. 28-1830),
charges A$34 single, A$40 double.

Transwell's Commercial Hotel, 30 Ford St. (tel. 28-1480),
118 years old, has toilets-down-the-hall rooms for A$25 single,
A$35 double, including breakfast. (Superb dinners are priced
from A$9.50 in the restaurant, and the pub serves A$6 counter
meals.) The **Empire Hotel**, Camp and High streets (tel.
28-1030), has a similar set-up with adequate rooms for A$15
single, A$25 double. Across the street from Transwell's, the
Youth Hostel (tel. 28-1425) is housed in the old Star Hotel.

Aside from Transwell's, you can dine well over the counter at
any of the town's four pubs. There's a Chinese restaurant, the
Chinese Village, on Camp Street, and many travelers enjoy
Rosemary's Coffee Shop on Ford Street.

DAY 7
BEECHWORTH TO MELBOURNE

After a morning tour of Beechworth, we'll visit the Brown
Brothers Winery at Millawa and stop in at Glenrowan, where
Ned Kelly, Australia's most notorious 19th Century bushranger,
made his "last stand." The afternoon's highlight is the Sir Colin
McKenzie Wildlife Sanctuary, an open-air reserve at Healesville
that is the best of its kind in the world. Arrive in Melbourne in
time for dinner.

Suggested Schedule	
8:00 a.m.	Breakfast in Beechworth, then explore the town and museum until about 10:30.
11:00 a.m.	Tour Brown Brothers Winery and sample the product.
11:45 a.m.	Dive into "Kelly Country" at the museums and roadside display in Glenrowan.
12:30 p.m.	Grab picnic fixings in Benalla and enjoy them on the banks of Lake Nillahcootie.
3:00 p.m.	Stroll for two hours among native Australian wildlife at the Sir Colin McKenzie Wildlife Sanctuary at Healesville.
6:30 p.m.	Arrive in Melbourne. Check into your hotel and head for a well-earned dinner on Lygon Street.

Beechworth Sightseeing Highlights
No fewer than 32 of Beechworth's buildings have been
classified or recorded by the National Trust. The best place to
start your exploration is the **Burke Memorial Museum**, on
Loch Street one-half block north of Camp Street. Established at
this site in 1863, it is one of Australia's finest small-town museums.
The collection is especially strong in pioneer history, the gold-
rush era, and memorabilia of the local Chinese community and
the Kelly Gang. A new gallery reproduces a 16-shop main street
of the mid-19th Century with retail shops, a doctor's office, an
assay office, a dance hall and other establishments. Open 2 to
4:30 p.m. Monday, 11 a.m. to 4:30 p.m. Friday, 9 a.m. to 4:30
p.m. all other days. (For the sake of our tour, the Friday hours
will hopefully be extended to 9 a.m. as well.) Admission is A$2.
   On leaving the Burke Museum, pick up a copy of the
lithographed brochure, "Beechworth Living History." Its map
will direct you to 34 points of interest in the Beechworth area,
most of them within easy walking distance. Among the proper-

ties administered by the National Trust are the **Carriage Museum**, behind Tanswell's Hotel, with an extensive collection of carriages and other turn-of-the-century vehicles, and the **Powder Magazine**, on Gorge Street at the west end of Camp Street, a fully restored brick building where gunpowder was cached for goldfield blasting in the 1850s. Both are open 10 a.m. to 4:30 p.m. daily from Boxing Day (Dec. 26) through May 31, then Sundays and holidays only the rest of the year.

Other buildings of special interest include the **H.M. Training Prison**, the brewery museum in the old **M.B. Cellars** and the **Chinese Burning Towers** at Beechworth Cemetery. If time allows, stop into the **Buckland Gallery**, perhaps the most interesting of several crafts shops in town.

The Route South

Milawa is little more than a crossroads on a secondary route midway between Beechworth and Glenrowan. But it's the site of Australia's finest wineries, the **Brown Brothers Vineyard and Winery**. John Francis Brown planted the first vines here in 1889, and four succeeding generations of Browns have carefully tended them. Sample some of the fermented grape juice—the Cabernet and Shiraz in red and the Chardonnay and Frontignac in white are particularly good—and take a bottle or two along for Melbourne's BYO restaurants.

Glenrowan is 21 km (13 miles) due west. Here, in 1880, an infamous 25-year-old outlaw named Ned Kelly and his three-man gang were cornered by police at the Glenrowan Inn. Kelly's companions, including his brother, were killed in a shootout; Ned himself was wounded and brought to trial in Melbourne, where he was hanged.

Over a period of fewer than three years before his capture, Kelly had cemented a reputation as a larcenous murderer. Yet his exploits—he was a superb horseman who wore a 97-pound hand-molded suit of armor to protect himself—so fascinated Australians of past and present that he has been immortalized in poems, plays, paintings, even a movie starring Mick Jagger.

You can't miss Glenrowan's Kelly kitsch, even if you want to. A Paul Bunyan-esque statue of Ned himself, garbed in his armor and toting a rifle, holds up a train emerging from a tunnel beside the Hume Highway. The so-called Glenrowan Tourist Centre contains the Ned Kelly Sound and Visual Museum, with a fully animated gunfight half-hourly from 10 a.m. to 4 p.m. daily (admission A$5); next door is a recreation of the cabin that Ned and his family called home; and everywhere you look there are Kelly T-shirts, books, records, cassette tapes, mugs, keychains, pennants and everything else imaginable. I can only advise you to keep your pennies in your pocket when you stop.

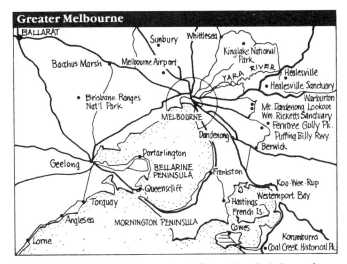

If you stop for groceries another 24 km (15 miles) down the road at **Benalla,** famous for its rose gardens from late October through March, you can take your picnic basket to **Lake Nillahcootie,** an oasis at the foot of Mount Samaria some 40 km (25 miles) south of town via the Midland Highway. After lunch, bypass Mansfield and pick up the Maroondah Highway, crossing the northern arm of serpentine Lake Eildon and continuing to charming Alexandra, the majestic Cathedral Range, and magnificent Maroondah fern forest. You'll arrive at the town of **Healesville** about 175 km (109 miles) from your picnic stop.

But don't stop in town. Follow the signs another 5 km southeast to the **Sir Colin McKenzie Wildlife Sanctuary,** often known simply as the "Healesville Sanctuary." This 79-acre reserve is home to nearly 2,000 mammals, birds and reptiles of 200 species, all of them Australian natives. Few are behind bars, and visitors have the opportunity to stroll freely through kangaroo enclosures and parrot aviaries. You'll find everything from koalas to platypuses, wombats to Tasmanian devils, emus to lyrebirds. The sanctuary is open 9 a.m. to 5 p.m. every day of the year (arrive before 3:30 if you want to see the platypus); admission is reasonable at A$5. A restaurant and gift shop are on the grounds. I consider the sanctuary—established in 1921 in this natural bushland setting—to be Australia's best wildlife park. Others apparently agree, for it is the most visited attraction in the state of Victoria.

If you stay at the sanctuary until the closing hour, you'll avoid most of the rush-hour traffic (it will be coming toward you, instead of with you) as you drive the final 62 km (40 miles) west of Melbourne. Just stay on the Maroondah Highway all the way into the city.

Melbourne Orientation

A stately and sophisticated metropolis of 2.9 million people, Melbourne (pronounced "Melb'n," not "Mel-born") is Australia's second city. Its elegant Victorian buildings and large Mediterranean and Asian population combine to give it a cosmopolitan Old World atmosphere. It's no accident that Melbourne is the shopping, dining, entertainment and sporting capital of the country.

Melbourne's role as Australia's financial center had more practical roots. Never a penal settlement, it was founded in 1835 by Europeans seeking to escape the more restrictive conditions on Tasmania. When the Victorian goldfields boomed in the 1850s, Melbourne became the center through which the riches were shipped. With their newfound wealth, Melbournians endowed their city with broad boulevards, beautiful parks and classically handsome architecture. And although Sydney, with its superior harbor and 50-year head start, was the country's best-known city, it was Melbourne that became Australia's first national capital (1901-1927) and the host of its only Olympic Games (1956).

With a latitude of 38 degrees south, about the same distance from the Equator as San Francisco is north, Melbourne has four distinct seasons . . . sometimes all in one day. Generalizations can be made—temperatures on summer days often range in the 80s Fahrenheit, while winter days average in the mid 50s—but the weather is definitely fickle, especially in the autumn months.

Melbourne's core is a neatly planned 1-by-2 km grid on the north bank of the Yarra River, with nine parallel streets running north-south and an equal number (five main streets and four widened alleys) crossing them from east to west. Swanston Street, which continues south across the Yarra, and Elizabeth Street, which connects to the Sydney-Canberra and Ballarat-Adelaide roads, are the main north-south thoroughfares. They are intersected by Flinders Street, flanking the river and the main metropolitan railway station; Collins Street, the address of most banks; Bourke Street, known for its shopping west of Swanston Street and its Chinatown east; Lonsdale Street, part of it called The Greek Precinct; and Latrobe Street, which extends east via Victoria Parade toward Healesville and the Dandenongs. You'll enter the city by this latter route.

City Transportation

The Metropolitan Transit System, known as the Met (tel. 617-0900), comprising rail and tram services, is Australia's best public transportation network. The trains stop at 235 stations within about a 40-km (25-mile) radius of the city center, and the web of electric trams (the only ones in Australia) fill in the gaps that the trains neglect. It seems as though you're never more than two blocks away from one. The system runs from 5:20 a.m. to 12:30 a.m. Monday to Saturday, 6:35 a.m. to 11:45 p.m. on Sunday. Single-ride tickets within the "Inner Neighborhood"—which includes almost all tourist attractions of note—are 70 cents; an unlimited travel two-hour ticket is $1.20; and an all-day ticket is $2.30. You can buy these and other tickets, as well as get free maps and more complete transit information, at Met depots, railway stations and the Royal Arcade kiosk between Bourke and Little Collins streets.

A new and integral part of The Met is the Melbourne Underground Rail Loop, a A$400 million project linking five stations around the perimeter of the central city.

Melbourne's international and main domestic airport is at Tullamarine, 19 km (12 miles) northwest of the city center. It is served by taxis and by special buses with direct connections to downtown hotels.

Where to Stay

At the top of the line, Melbourne has two outstanding hotels which eschew modern steel and concrete for the classic look: **Menzies at Rialto**, 459 Collins St. (tel. 62-0111), and **The Windsor**, 103 Spring St. (tel. 63-0261). The Menzies has created an atrium out of two neo-Gothic 19th Century buildings, while The Windsor, opposite the old Parliament House, has retained its century-old feeling right down to the stained-glass dome lights in the dining room. Both cost A$110 and up.

At the top of the moderate price bracket, I like the centrally-located **Hotel Australia**, 266 Collins St. (tel. 653-0401), which still feels like it must have when it was U.S. Gen. Jonathan Wainwright's Second World War headquarters. One columnist described it as a hotel of "rescinded greatness." Its comfortable rooms go for $30 double ($70 for card-carrying AAA members). But parking is a hassle, so those with cars might prefer the **Downtowner Motel**, 66 Lygon St., Carlton (tel. 347-7733), doubles $53, close to Melbourne's best restaurant strip; or in East Melbourne, the **Albert Heights Apartments**, 83 Albert St., with one-bedroom kitchen suites for $68 (AAA members $58).

In the economy class, try the **Victoria Hotel**, 215 Little Collins St. (tel. 63-0441), downtown; or the charming **Magnolia Court**, 101 Powlett St., East Melbourne (tel. 417-2782), facing Fitzroy Gardens. For budget lodging, the city's two **YHA youth hostels** are within a block of each other in North Melbourne, 3 km from downtown. The larger of the two, 76 Chapman St. (tel. 328-3595), charges A$7.50 a head for its 50 double rooms. The

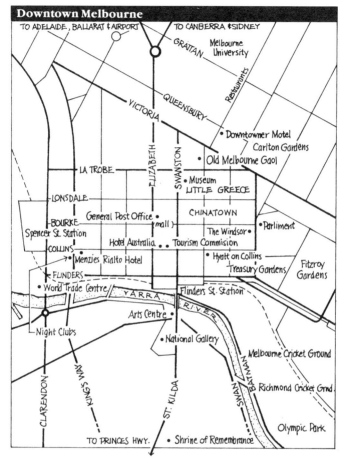

older dormitory-style hostel at 500 Abbotsford St. (tel. 328-2880) charges $8. You can also find good accommodation year-round at the University of Melbourne's **International House**, 241 Royal Parade, Parkville (tel. 347-2351), about 4 km north of downtown, with single rooms and shared baths.

Where to Eat

Melbourne is an epicure's delight, a city with a multitude of excellent restaurants to appeal to any palate. . .and any wallet. This is partly a response to its attitude of self-importance, but perhaps even more a result of its broad base of ethnic diversity. The Greeks (only Athens and Thessalonika have larger Greek populations than Melbourne), Italians, Yugoslavs, Turks, Lebanese, Chinese and Vietnamese, in particular, have left their marks on Melbourne's dining habits.

There are several restaurant "strips" in Melbourne, but perhaps none so acclaimed as Lygon Street in Carlton, a short stroll up Russell Street from the city center. The main Italian neighborhood of Melbourne, this is the place for pasta and pizzas. **Toto's** (No. 101), **El Gambero** (No. 215), **Il Gusto (No. 256) and Tiamo's** (No. 303) are among the best known, all serving good meals for less than A$10 per person. But this district is no longer strictly Italian; check the side streets for Japanese food at the **Samurai**, 210 Drummond St.; Mexican at **Cha Chi's**, 161 Nicholson St.; Malay and Chinese at the **Bali House**, 157 Elgin St.; vegetarian at **Shakahari**, 329 Lygon St.

Melbourne's most famous restaurant, **Mietta's**, is downtown near the deluxe international hotels—at 7 Alfred Place (between Exhibition and Russell streets off Collins street). Put out a A$100 for two, and you'll get an exquisite continental dinner with equally generous service. But you can eat well in the city center without breaking your budget. You can't go wrong in Chinatown (Little Bourke Street east of Swanston) if you check out the menus in the windows and see where the locals are eating. I like the **Bamboo House**, 47 Little Bourke St., for Mandarin cuisine and the **Empress of China**, 120 Little Bourke St., for Cantonese.

The Greek restaurants on Lonsdale Street east of Swanston are also excellent. Try **Stalactites** (open 24 hours) at Londsdale and Russell Streets. You'll find even more Greek eateries—plus a slew of Vietnamese places—in the Richmond district east of the city center. Similarly, there's a Turkish dining strip on Sydney Road in Brunswick, north of downtown.

A personal favorite for a splurge is **Percy's**, 384 Punt Road, South Yarra, an innovative BYO spot with a blackboard menu that changes daily. Other local choices include **Cafe Lisboa** (Portuguese), 413 Brunswick St., Fitzroy; **Costa Brava** (Spanish), 36 Johnston St., Fitzroy; and **Isabella's**, a bistro at Russell and Little Collins Streets downtown.

For lunch, **Jimmy Watson's Wine Bar**, 333 Lygon St., is hard to beat for good, cheap cuisine in an amiable atmosphere. On the south side, the **Station Hotel**, Chapel and Peel streets in Prahran, has counter meals for as little as A$3.

With some 2,000 restaurants in Melbourne, there's never a fear about where to eat. So sophisticated is the city in its dining habits, there's a white-linen restaurant aboard a tram, and another on a double-decker bus!

Helpful Hints
The **Victorian Tourism Center** (tel. 602-9444),
known as "Victour," handles tourist information on Melbourne
city as well as Victoria. It is centrally located at 230 Collins St.
and is open 9 a.m. to 5 p.m. Monday to Friday, 9 a.m. to noon
Saturday. There is also a **Melbourne Tourism Authority** (tel.
654-2288) on the 20th floor of Nauru House, 80 Collins St.

The **General Post Office**, at the corner of Bourke and
Elizabeth streets, is open 8 a.m. to 6 p.m. Monday to Friday.
Most city banks are open 9:30 a.m. to 4 p.m. Monday to Thursday, 9:30 a.m. to 5 p.m. Friday. Shop hours vary, but you can
generally expect downtown merchants to be open from 9 a.m.
to 5:30 p.m. Monday to Thursday, 9 a.m. to 9 p.m. Friday, 9 a.m.
to noon Saturday.

There's an **American Consulate** in South Melbourne at 24
Albert Road (tel. 699-2244), and a **Canadian Consulate**
downtown at 151 Flinders St. (tel. 63-8431).

In case of emergencies, dial 000.

DAY 8
MELBOURNE

Explore the city today. Wander through ethnic neighborhoods, sophisticated shopping arcades, the high-brow banking district. The Old Gaol and the National Museum of Victoria are worthy stops. Don't miss the beautiful Victorian Arts Centre or the nation's best botanic gardens. But don't overdo the sightseeing. Here in sports-crazy Melbourne, try to soak up some local culture by attending (depending on the season) a "footie" (Australian rules football) match, cricket test or horse race.

Suggested Schedule

9:00	A good way to see Melbourne is to start at the north end of downtown and work your way south on Swanston Street. First stop is Victoria Market, where rows of fresh fruit vendors can supply a juicy breakfast.
10:00	The Old Melbourne Gaol and Penal Museum.
10:45	The National Museum of Victoria, last resting place of Phar Lap.
11:45	Explore the Greek Precinct and Chinatown, stopping in one or the other for lunch.
1:00	Bourke Street Mall and shopping arcades.
2:00	Collins Street, Melbourne's true "Golden Mile."
2:30	Victorian Arts Centre, the largest multi-arts complex in the world.
3:30	The National Gallery of Victoria, Australia's finest art museum.
5:00	Royal Botanic Gardens.
6:00	Dinner.
7:00	Join the fanatic throngs at a sports event. There's always something going on Saturday night.
10:00	Climax your day with a little nightlife.

Sightseeing Highlights
▲**Victoria Market** is a large open-air market near the intersection of Queen and Victoria Streets. (The main entrance is off Franklin Street.) On Tuesday, Friday and Saturday mornings starting at 6:00 a.m., it's a multicultural potourri of fruit and vegetable vendors, while on Sundays from 9:00 a.m. to 4:00 p.m., it turns into an enormous flea market especially popular among craft and antique dealers.

▲▲**The Old Melbourne Gaol and Penal Museum**, Russel Street near Lygon, is a dank and morbid but fascinating relic of the days (1841 to 1929) when men were men and felons were hanged. Here are the gallows and isolation cells known and feared by hundreds of convicts, including the notorious bushranger Ned Kelly. The jail exhibits Kelly's handmade armor and his "death mask," created for phrenologists to study possible clues to his deviant behavior. Open 10:00 a.m. to 5:00 p.m. daily except Sunday. Admission $3.

▲▲**The National Museum of Citoria**, Swanston and LaTrobe Streets, has an excellent exhibit of state history, a new science and technology section, plus good natural history and ethnography displays. Deep within its chambers, however, is the reason so many Australians consider this a religious site. Phar Lap, generally regarded as the greatest racehorse that ever lived, stands within a glass display case—at least, his stuffed skin does. (His heart is in Canberra.) The steed won an incredible 37 of his 51 starts, earning over A$133,000, before dying a mysterious death in Menlo Park, California, in 1932 at the age of 5½. (If you saw the 1983 Australian movie, you know all this.) The museum is open from 10:00 a.m. to 4:45 p.m. Monday to Saturday, 2:00 to 4:45 p.m. Sunday. Free admission.

The Greek Precinct of Lonsdale Street, from Swanston to Russell Street, is being upgraded to emphasize the outdoor cafes and colorful specialist shops. The traditional Edwardian character of the buildings has been maintained. If you're here in March or April, chances are you'll catch a festival.

▲**Chinatown**—two blocks from Swanston Street to Exhibition Street, bissected by Little Bourke Street—is linked to the Greek Precinct via Heffernan Lane. Chinese have lived in this neighborhood since 1854. The opium dens have long since closed, but many of the butchers, bakers and candlemakers still ply trades learned from their forefathers. Today, the restaurants and shops on Little Bourke and its side lanes, especially Celestial Avenue, comprise the most interesting Chinatown in the Southern Hemisphere. The Museum of Chinese Australian History, 22 Cohen Place, contains photographs, artifacts, and an audio-visual presentation. Open weekdays except Tuesday 10:00 a.m. to 4:30 p.m., weekends noon to 4:30 p.m.

▲**Bourke Street Mall** is the shopping center of Australia's shopping capital. The Myer Emporium, for example, is the world's second largest department store (after Marshall Field's in Chicago), taking up a good portion of two city blocks on the north side of the mall. Next door to it is David Jones, Australia's answer to J.C. Penney. The south side of the mall is interlaced by a maze of delightfully restored shopping arcades. In particular, check out the Royal Arcade, with its campy 1892 clock depicting Gog and Magog striking the time.

There are several other great shopping streets in the suburbs. Armadale High Street is packed with antique, craft, book and clothing shops; Chapel Street and Toorak Road are the hubs of a glitzy high-fashion neighborhood in South Yarra; and St. Kilda's Acland Street is famous for its pastry shops.

Parliament House, on Spring Street at the east end of Bourke, was built in 1856 and served as the federal Parliament until the provisional house in Canberra opened in 1927. It still serves as Victoria's state assembly chambers. Guided tours are offered at 10:00 a.m., 11:00 a.m., and 2:00 p.m. Monday through Friday.

▲**Collins Street** is where the nation's most important financial institutions are housed, mnay of them in Victorian gold-rush masterpieces spliced between steel-and-glass skyscrapers. If you're here on a weekday, take a walking tour, starting at the ANZ Banking Museum (open 9:30 a.m. to 4:00 p.m. Monday to Friday) in the basement of the Australia-New Zealand Bank, 386 Collins St. Then step inside the institution upstairs for a look-around, and also have a peek into the Bank of New Zealand (No., 395), National Australian Bank (No. 335) and Westpac (No. 331). The Melbourne Stock Exchange, 351 Collins St., has a third floor visitors gallery with a broad view of the trading floor. It's open Monday to Friday from 9:00 a.m. to noon and 2:00 to 5:00 p.m.

▲▲**The Victorian Arts Centre** is modern Melbourne's pride and joy. The city proudly trumpets that this is "the largest arts center in the world." Indeed, the complex—completed only 1985—includes a 2,600-seat concert hall, three theatres for opera, ballet and drama, three licensed restaurants, an art shop, a museum, and the adjoining National Gallery of Victoria. Its 500-foot Eiffel-like spire, which towers over the Yarra River beside St. Kilda Road, can be seen for miles around.

A variety of tours are offered to show off the Centre and its unusual architecture. There are morning tea tours weekdays for A$10, or luncheon tours for A$18. Evening tours, starting promptly at 5:00 p.m. Monday to Friday, include dinner and a show for A$45. Short tours at 10:30 a.m. daily cost A$2.75; Sunday backstage tours are A$6.

The Melbourne Symphony Orchestra often plays free lunch-time concerts, and every Friday from 5:00 to 7:00 p.m., there's a free jazz show in the basement Monsanto Lounge. Bookings should be made for all other performances and tours by calling 617-8211.

▲**The Performing Arts Museum**, in the concert hall, is highly regarded internationally. Its changing exhibits range from silent films or horror movies to recreations of Dame Nellie Melba's operatic recordings. Open 11:00 a.m. to 5:00 p.m. Monday to Friday, noon to 5:00 p.m. Saturday. Admission A$1.10.

▲▲▲**The National Gallery of Victoria**, on the south side of
the Victorian Arts Centre at 180 St. Kilda Road, was Australia's
first public art gallery (founded in 1861) and is still the finest in
the Southern Hemisphere. Its most popular galleries to overseas
visitors are those of Aboriginal and Oceanic art and of Australian
art, especially featuring its noted Heidelberg school of late 19th
Century impressionists—Tom Roberts, Arthur Streeton, Fred-
erick McCubbin and Charles Condon. Its collection of more
than 50,000 works also includes divisions of European, British
and American art, Asian art, pre-Columbian art, costumes and
textiles, decorative arts, prints and drawings, and photography.
Open daily except Monday from 10:00 a.m. to 5:00 p.m. Admission A$1.20.
▲▲**The Royal Botanic Gardens**, a half-kilometer stroll south
and east of the Arts Centre, are considered one of the world's
best landscaped gardens. More than 12,000 plant species thrive
in the 88 acres of lawns, garden beds and ornamental lakes,
along with over 50 species of birds.

Adjacent to the gardens is the much larger **King's Domain**,
containing the massive Shrine of Remembrance war memorial;
the circa-1840 LaTrobe's Cottage, Victoria's original government
house (open daily 10:00 a.m. to 4:30 p.m., admission A$1.60);
and the Sidney Myer Music Bowl, an outdoor amphitheatre by
summer, a covered public ice rink by winter. The 11-km Yarra
River Bikeway starts here; bicycles can be hired opposite the
Botanic Gardens in Alexandra Avenue from 11:00 a.m. to dusk
weekends and holidays.

Melbourne's other famous parks include **Fitzroy Gardens**, in
East Melbourne between Wellington Parade and Albert Street.
Its highlight is Captain Cook's Cottage, transported here from
Yorkshire, England, in 1934 and reassembled (open 9:00 a.m. to
5:00 p.m. daily, admission 80 cents). The adjacent **Treasury
Gardens**, facing Spring Street, contain a John Kennedy mem-
orial. **Carlton Gardens**, Victoria Street opposite Spring, contain the Royal Exhibition Buildings built in 1880 for the inaugu-
tion of the commonwealth of Australia. **Albert Park**, between
South Melbourne and St. Kilda, has a large lake with boat rentals.
▲**The Royal Melbourne Zoo**, on Elliott Avenue in Royal Park
(north of the city center), is the third oldest zoo on Earth. The
aviary, they say, is bigger than Paris' Cathedral of Notre Dame.
The 55 acres have recently been relandscaped, with most of the
336 species now in simulated natural environments. Open 1:00
a.m. to 5:30 p.m. daily. Admission A$4.40.
▲**Como House** (1855), on Como Avenue in South Yarra, and
Ripponlea (1887), on Hotham Street in Elsternwick, are two
beautiful colonial mansions set in spacious suburban gardens.
Both have been refurnished with the trappings of the Victorian

elite; both are open daily 10:00 a.m. to 5:00 p.m. and charge
A$3.50 admission. (Repponlea has limited winter hours.)
▲**The Polly Woodside**, anchored in the Yarra River at Nor-
manby Road and Phayer Street in South Melbourne, is a
restored iron-hulled Irish sailing vessel now finding new duty
as the focus of a maritime museum. Open Monday to Friday,
10:00 a.m. to 4:00 p.m., and weekends noon to 5:00 p.m. Admission A$4.

The City Explorer Bus (tel. 598-5355) leaves the Flinders
Street Station hourly from 10:00 a.m. to 4:00 p.m. every day but
Monday. It stops at Captain Cook's Cottage, the Old Gaol, the
National Museum, the Polly Woodside and the National Gallery.
One-day tickets for the on-again, off-again loop are A$5.

Melbourne Nightlife

Melbourne doesn't have any equivalent to Sydney's King Cross.
Its nightlife is spread across the metropolis, from downtown to
the suburbs. St. Kilda, a short hop south of the city center,
tends to be the hippest area; Richmond (east) and Carlton
(north) can also be lively.

The Friday morning edition of *The Age* gives full listings of
the entertainment week ahead. Rock music dominates the
scene, but you'll find far more jazz and acoustic music in
Melbourne than in other big cities.

The only thing approaching a downtown "strip" is King
Street from Collins to Flinders. In one block, there's live rock at
Inflation and the **Melbourne Underground**; discos at the
Hippodrome and the **York Butter Factory**; cabaret at **Laz-
zars International**; jazz and folk at the **Grainstore Tavern**.
Some of the nightspots are open all night—you can rage 'til
7:00 a.m.

The **Limerick Arms Hotel** in South Melbourne and the
Bridge Hotel in Richmond are two of the city's best venues for
live jazz, while the Moomba Hotel in North Melbourne is good
for country sounds Wednesday through Friday.

The No. 1 meeting spot in town, at this writing, was the new
Hyatt on Collins, at the corner of Russell Street. The casual
bars and restaurants in the basement of its atrium are packed
from the off-work hours to closing. **Zanie's**, a trendie bar-
bistro at Lonsdale and Russell Streets, draws a good crowd. The
Sherlock Holmes Inn, 421 Collins St., attracts lovers of traditional British pubs. Gays like the appropriately named **Mandate**
in St. Kilda.

Young and Jackson's, 1 Swanston St. at Flinders, is
Melbourne's most famous pub and one of its oldest. Since the
Melbourne Exhibition of 1880, it has displayed above its bar an

oil painting of "Chloe" —a full-length nude that once shocked Victorian sentiments. For symphony, theatre, opera, ballet, etc., the obvious first choice is the **Victorian Arts Centre** (see "Sightseeing Highlights"). Other major stages downtown—**Her Majesty's Theatre**, 219 Exhibition St., and the **Princess Theatre**, 163 Spring St.—are within three blocks of each other. This section of downtown Melbourne, along Bourke Street between Spring and Swanston, is also the location of most cinema houses for first-run movies.

Melbourne hosts two major festivals during the year. Moomba, in March, is the Mardi Gras Down Under. Gian Carlo Menotti's Spoleto Arts Festival, in September/October, is a more sedate but culturally fulfilling event.

DAY 9
BALLARAT

Ballarat is synonymous with two subjects near and dear to
Australians' hearts: gold and independence. Today's outing
covers both ends of this historic Victorian city—Sovereign Hill,
the country's No. 1 theme park, faithful to its 1850s heyday; and
the Eureka Stockade, site (in 1854) of a much-heralded rebellion
unique in Australian history.

Suggested Schedule	
8:00	Leave Melbourne, heading west on the Great Western Freeway (Highway 8).
10:00	Arrive in Ballarat. Sovereign Hill is the town's central attraction. Plan to spend several hours, including lunch.
2:00	Cross the street to the Gold Museum.
3:00	Relive the glory of the Eureka Stockade.
4:00	See Montrose Cottage, the Botanic Gardens or another of Ballarat's attractions.
5:30	Head back to Melbourne for dinner and rest.

Ballarat Orientation
Victoria's second largest city with a population of 90,000,
Ballarat is located 113 km (70 miles) west of Melbourne. It was
founded by gold diggers in 1851 and quickly became an
Eldorado, with fortune hunters from around the world coverg-
ing on the settlement after hearing fairy tales about gold nug-
gets being plucked off the streets. In fact, the argonauts had to
work for their gold, but they pulled an estimated 20 million
ounces from the hills before the last mine closed in 1918. At today's prices, that would be worth about US $9.4 billion.
    Much of the money that gold wrought was poured into con-
structing a beautiful town on the frontier. With the opening of
the railroad in 1962, Ballarat became the gateway to western
Victoria, and its future was assured. Today it is known for its
gardens and art galleries as much as for its historic sites.
    The Western Highway—Stuart Street through most of
downtown—bisects Ballarat into northern and southern halves.
The Gold Centre Tourist Centre (tel. 053/32-2694), on Lydiard
Street outside the railway station, is two blocks north of the
highway near the business center of town. Sovereign Hill is
perhaps a mile south of the center on Bradshaw Street (just off
Main Road). The Eureka Stockade, exhibition and diorama are
on Stawell Street, just south of the Western Highway at the east
end of Ballarat.

City Transportation
If you don't drive to Ballarat—if you perchance took the train
or bus from Melbourne—you can shuttle to the town's attractions on the Shuttlebus (tel 31-2655). Seven loop trips a day are
operated around the city, taking in Sovereign Hill and the Eureka Stockade. You can board between 9:30 a.m. and 4:00 p.m.
at the Tourism Centre at the railway station, disembark and
reboard wherever you choose along the route for A$8. The
Shuttlebus also travels between Ballarat and Melbourne's Tullamarine airport three or four times daily, with A$30 covering
round-trip transportation plus admission charges at Sovereign
Hill and the Eureka Exhibition.

Sightseeing Highlights
▲▲▲**Sovereign Hill** is a place of living history, an authentic
recreation of the Australia's most important gold-mining
township of the 1850s. Operated by a non-profit local association whose 200 volunteers dress in period costume, the park
has three main sections. In the Red Hill Gully Diggings (faithful
to the period 1851-1855), brightly dressed miners emerge from
their tents and mud huts to show visitors how to pan for alluvial
gold. In the Goldmining Township (1854-1861), horse-drawn
coaches roll past 29 separate working businesses—among them
a blacksmith, coachbuilder, tinsmith, confectioner, printer, pot-
ter and furniture maker with a steam-driven lathe. In the Mining
Museum (1860-1918), you can travel underground to learn how
quartz reef mining was done, while above you a thunderous
stamper battery crushes the gold-bearing quartz.
    Main Street is Sovereign Hill's core. You can dine in style at the
New York Bakery or the Licensed United States Hotel. (Takeaway
food and barbecue supplies are also available in the Township.)
You can attend comedy sketches in the Victoria Theatre, or try
your hand at skittles in the Empire Bowling Saloon.
    Low-cost accommodation is available at Government Camp,
a recreated 1850s military barracks on a hill overlooking the
Township. Though the buildings might appear old, they're comfortably modern within. Families of four can stay for $35 a
night (for four); there's also a YHA youth hostel on the site.
    The park is open daily (except Christmas) from 9:30 a.m. to
5:00 p.m. Admission is A$8; for A$10, you can get a Gold Pass
which inclues a coach ride and admission to the adjacent Gold
Museum.
▲▲**The Gold Museum**, on Bradshaw Street across from the
Sovereign Hill car park, is a worthy adjunct to the theme park.
Its historical exhibits, while emphasizing the gold rush era
and Eureka Stockade rebellion, also recall central Victoria's
Aboriginal history and the creation of its wool industry. The

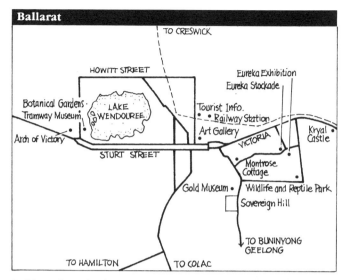

Ballarat

TO CRESWICK
HOWITT STREET
Eureka Exhibition
Eureka Stockade
Botanical Gardens
Tramway Museum
LAKE WENDOUREE
Tourist Info.
Railway Station
Art Gallery
VICTORIA
Arch of Victory
Kryal Castle
STURT STREET
Montrose Cottage
Gold Museum
Wildlife and Reptile Park
Sovereign Hill
TO BUNINYONG GEELONG
TO HAMILTON
TO COLAC

Gold Pavilion displays important private collections of rare gold coins from around the world and turn-of-the-century Chinese artifacts. Open 9:30 a.m. to 5:30 p.m. daily except Christmas. Admission A$1.50.

▲▲**Eureka Stockade** is a name with the same ring to Australians as the Alamo has to Texans. Like Davy Crockett, Jim Bowie et. al., the miners lost this battle—but they won the war.

Mercilessly taxed and oppressed by the British colonial administration, the diggers made a gallant stand for their democratic rights. The climax came on Dec. 3, 1854, when government troopers attacked a stockaded position held by miners near the Eureka diggings. Six troopers and 22 miners died. The tragedy shocked Victoria's colonial leaders into introducing long-awaited reforms in the goldfields. Within a year, two leaders of the revolt were elected to the first Victorian Parliament under a new constitution.

Today, at the Eureka Street Parklands (at the corner of Stawell Street), the rebellion is remembered by a memorial, a reconstructed stockade and a diorama of the incident. More impressive is the Eureka Exhibition, catty-corner from the memorial at Eureka and Kline Streets, with a series of computer-controlled scenes depicting various episodes of the revolt. Open daily 9:00 a.m. to 6:00 p.m.

The miners' famous Southern Cross banner flew over the stockade for only five days—yet Aussies hold it in the same esteem as Americans do Betsy Ross' "13 stars on a field of blue."

The Eureka flag can be seen in the Ballarat Fine Art Gallery, 40 Lydiard St. (near the Tourism Centre).

▲**Montrose Cottage**, 111 Eureka St., is the last original bluestone masonry cottage surviving from 1850² Ballarat. Classified by the National Trust, it contains the small Eureka Museum of Social History. Open daily 9:30 a.m. to 5:30 p.m.

The 100-acre **Botanic Gardens** encompass Lake Wendouree on the northwest side of Ballarat. Prime Ministers Avenue, within the gardens, is flanked by bronze busts of all Australian prime ministers, right up through the leader in 1987, Bob Hawke.

Kryal Castle, 8 km east of Ballarat on the Western Highway, is a curiosity: a recreated medieval castle where costumed actors reenact the life and pageantry of the Middle Ages. There's jousting, sword-fighting, even the occasional hanging, and a tavern where a medieval banquet is held every Saturday night. Open 9:30 a.m. to 5:30 p.m. daily except Christmas.

Golda's World of Dolls, 148 Eureka St., displays more than 2,000 rare, antique and period-costumed dolls from all over the world. Open 1:00 to 5:00 p.m. Monday to Thursday, 10:00 a.m. to 5:00 p.m. weekends and holidays. Closed Fridays.

The Arch of Victory, at the west end of Ballarat marks the beginning of the tree-lined, 21 km-long Avenue of Honour to the men and women of Ballarat who volunteered for active service abroad during World War One.

DAY 10

DANDENONG RANGES AND PHILLIP ISLAND

The "Blue Dandenongs," a relaxing day trip on the east side of Melbourne, contain many beautiful gardens, a unique sculpture forest, a park noted for its lyrebirds, and various other attractions. The day's highlight comes at dusk, when hundreds or thousands of tiny fairy penguins parade from the sea to their burrows, up a concrete walkway as hundreds of flash cameras click away.

Suggested Schedule	
9:00	Leave Melbourne as soon as rush hour has ended.
10:15	Stroll through the William Ricketts Sanctuary, with its environmentally oriented sculptures of Aboriginal Mother Nature theme.
11:00	Visit Mount Dandenong Observatory to gaze at the high-rises of Melbourne in the distance.
11:30	The pretty artisans' village of Olinda is also the site of the National Rhododendron Gardens.
12:15	Lunchtime at a tearoom in Olinda or Sassafras.
1:00	The elusive Lyrebird runs free in Sherbrooke Forest Park.
2:00	Take a quick swim at Emerald Lake Park or visit a model railway museum near the terminus of the Puffing Billy steam train from Belgrave.
4:30	Arrive at Phillip Island for the penguin parade. The parade occurs about dusk, so the exact time varies from season to season.
After Dark	Return to Melbourne, stopping for dinner en route.

(Note: On Sundays, these roads are always packed by local day-trippers. Plan to skip a couple of attractions in the Dandenongs to reach Phillip Island on time.)

The Dandenong Ranges
The forested mountains east of Melbourne aren't especially high—Mount Dandenong itself is only 633 meters (2,076 feet)—but that's enough to lift them above the occasional smog of Port Phillip Bay and endow them with a rich plant and animal life. A surprising number of artists and nature lovers

choose to live in the Dandenongs and commute 60 to 90 minutes (each way) to the city daily.

The fastest route to the Dandenong Ranges is to head back east on the Maroondah Highway, as to Heaseville, but turn right at Ringwood on the well-marked Mount Dandenong Road. A drive of about an hour from the city brings you to Montrose, at the northern end of the Mount Dandenong Tourist Road. Sightseeing highlights of the Dandenongs, moving down the road from north to south, include:

▲▲**William Ricketts Sanctuary**. Like J.R.R. Tolkien gone mad, Ricketts—who celebrated his 88th birthday in 1987—is an eccentric musician-turned-artist-turned environmental radical. His enchanting clay sculptures decorate a lovely fern forest on the slopes of Mont Dandenong; indeed, they are a part of the forest, carefully melded to existing trees, rocks and brooks. All of Ricketts' work has Aboriginal and spiritual overtones. His more recent sculptures also make fierce animal rights and anti-exploitation statements. "Being part of nature," he writes, "we are brothers to the birds and trees. Will you then join with us in the sacredness of beauty?" Open 10:00 a.m. to 5:00 p.m. daily. Admission A$2.50.

▲**Mount Dandenong Observatory**. Outside the mountain-top restaurant and tea room are a roadside observation area and a handful of coin-in-the-slot telescopes to gaze across at the metropolis of Melbourne in the near west.

Edward Henty Cottage. A pioneer museum and antique shop occupy the former home of one of the Dandenongs' early residents. Located a short distance above Olinda. Admission to the museum is A$1.50.

▲**Olinda**. Art galleries and small restaurants specializing in midday Devonshire teas line the road around this picturesque village. It's worth getting out of the car and walking around.

▲**National Rhodendron Gardens**. Rhody lovers go bananas over these Olinda gardens in the spring and summer. By autumn, there's not much to look at. Admission A$3.00.

▲**Sherbrooke Forest Park**. Taken any of the tranquil trails through this lush nature preserve and you're likely to see or hear the lyrebird, a grouse-sized ground bird with a long, lacy, peacock-like tail used in courtship demonstrations. The lyrebird is remarkable for its ability to mimic almost any sound it hears, from other birds to machinery. (I was once awakened while camping by the sound of a logging truck. There were no logging roads nearby, but there were lyrebirds.) Also in the forest are Sherbrook Falls, Alfred Nicholas Memorial Gardens and four picnic grounds with barbecue facilities.

Fern Tree Gully National Park. Just above the town of Upper Ferntree Gully, this small park encompassing a valley of beautiful fern trees offers pleasant walks and colorful rosellas galore.

Belgrave. Another artists community, somewhat larger than Olinda, Belgrave lies at a major junction in the Dandenongs. It's best known as the depot for Puffing Billy.

▲▲**Puffing Billy**. Australia's best-known narrow-gauge steam railroad—built in 1900 to carry farm produce—packs its wooden cars with weekend and holiday day-trippers year-round, daily during school vacations (except on days of total fire ban). Puffing Billy typically leaves Belgrave at 10:30 a.m. on its 13-km (8-mile), 40-minute run up and down the ridges to Emerald Lake Park, returning at 12:40 p.m. There are additional runs on weekends. Round-trip fare is A$8.20 for adults, A$5.50 for kids. (Call 870-8411 for timetable specifics.) There's a Steam Museum at Menzies Creek, open 11:00 a.m. to 5:00 p.m. Sundays and holidays, with a collection of early locomotives. We won't have time for a ride on Puffing Billy in this itinerary, but you may enjoy it if you have an extra day or two in Melbourne.

▲**Emerald Lake Park**. A spacious, well-kept park surrounding a lake popular with swimmers and fisherman, this is the eastern terminus of Puffing Billy. Above the station is a pavilion containing Australia's largest model railway: over 2 kilometers of track. A youth hostel stands near the park's entrance. In Emerald village are many quaint shops and craft galleries.

Phillip Island

It will take about 30 minutes to drive from Emerald Lake Park to Pakenham, and another 90 minutes to follow the South Gippsland and Bass highways south to San Remo, at the east end of the 604-meter (2,100-foot) Narrows Bridge connecting Phillip Island to the Victorian mainland.

Phillip Island's main attraction, one of the outstanding sights in all of Australia, is the **Penguin Parade** at Summerland Beach, near the island's southwestern tip, every night of the year. A colony of fairy penguins numbering in the thousands spend most of their days fishing in Bass Strait, returning at dusk to their burrows in the sand dunes at this protected reserve. Bright lights illuminate the beach as the penguins straggle in to land and up a concrete walkway, while a crowd of camera-happy tourists quietly view from controlled areas behind a wire fence. These little (foot-high) birds are so cuddly-looking that it's hard not to smile as you watch them waddle through their nightly ritual, apparently oblivious to all the human attention.

You can buy tickets to the viewing area (for A$5) at the Penguin Reserve office beginning 30 minutes before the parade, or at the Phillip Island Information Centre near San Remo, open daily 9:00 a.m. to 5:00 p.m. (Don't tell anyone, but there's

another nightly penguin parade, albeit smaller, off St. Kilda
Parade near downtown Melbourne.)

The penguins aren't the only wild denizens of 25,000-acre
Phillip Island. Koalas roam freely in the eucalyptus groves of
Oswin Roberts Reserve. Fur seals maintain an offshore colony
on **The Nobbies**, a 50 million-year-old volcanic rock stack: up
to 4,500 of the marine mammals breed here in November and
December. Mutton birds (short-tailed shearwaters) nest on Cape
Woolamai, the island's southeasternmost point.

Len Lukey Memorial Museum and Gardens at Smith's
Beach, about halfway along the south shore, exhibits a good
collection of vintage cars and racing vehicles from a late-
lamented motor racing track. The island also features dairy and
shell museums, a center for wool artisans, three chicory kilns, a
historic homestead on Churchill Island (connected to Phillip
Island by a footbridge at Newhaven), a small zoo, a large
blowhole, a cavern, golf courses and other standard resort
amenities.

Cowes, the island's main town (on the north shore), has am-
ple accommodation and eating places. (In summer, it's best to
dine before the parade, because the restaurants close early.)

DAY 11

ALICE SPRINGS

Drop your car at Melbourne's Tullamarine Airport and catch a morning flight to Alice Springs. You'll have all afternoon and evening to explore this Outback oasis. Visit the Old Telegraph Station and the Royal Flying Doctor Service. To climax your day, ride a camel down the dry Todd River bed to dinner at a desert winery.

Suggested Schedule	
9:00	Return car to Tullamarine Airport.
10:00	Depart Melbourne on Ansett Flight #77 for Alice Springs.
12:20	Arrive at Alice Springs.
1:00	Check into your accommodation.
1:30	Orient yourself at the Anzac Hill viewpoint.
1:45	See the Old Telegraph Station.
2:30	Visit the School of the Air.
3:00	Drop in on the Royal Flying Doctor Service.
4:00	Take a camel to dinner.
9:00	Return to Alice Springs.

Leaving Melbourne
Flemington Road leads north into the Calder Highway, taking you to Melbourne International Airport at Tullamarine. Arrive well before your flight departure to turn in your rental car.

Ansett Flight #77 operates non-stop to Alice Springs (leaving Melbourne at 10:00 a.m.) only on Tuesday and Thursdays. On any other day of the week, you must plan your departure around 7:30 a.m. on either Ansett or Australian Airlines. Both carriers route daily flights to Alice Springs via Adelaide.

Alice Springs Orientation
With a rapidly growing population of about 25,000, ''The Alice'' is the biggest town for more than 800 miles in any direction. A desert oasis, it is situated in the midst of the MacDonnel Ranges, almost exactly in the geographic center of the continent. Australians call this area ''The Centre'' (or ''The Red Centre'' because of the unusual color of its soil).

Founded in 1872 as a station on the Overland Telegraph Line between Adelaide and Darwin, it got its name when station master Charles Todd dubbed a permanent waterhole in the bed of the usually dry Todd River ''Alice Springs'' after his wife.

When the railroad came through in 1929, the population was still only 200. A road from Adelaide was completed about 1940; only in April 1987 was the final link paved. The population didn't reach 1,000 until the 1950s or 5,000 until the 1970s. Modern tourism, however, has contributed to a boom throughout the Northern Territory, especially in The Alice.

The central business district is a compact 12 square blocks between the highway and the Todd River, bounded by Wills Terrace on the north and Stott Terrace on the south. The Todd Street Mall, recently made a pedestrians-only thoroughfare, stretches for two blocks from Gregory Terrace to Wills Terrace a block west of the river and is regarded as the center of town. (It is bisected by Parsons Street, and is paralleled to the west by Hartley and Bath Streets and to the east by Leichhardt Terrace overlooking the river.)

The word river, by the way, is a misnomer. To be called a "local" in Alice Springs, one must have seen the Todd flow its length three times. Some 20-year residents are still waiting to become locals. The river is completely dry most of the year.

The Northern Territory Government Tourist Bureau, 51 Todd St. at Parsons St. (tel. 52-1299), has a wide selection of maps, brochures and other information, incuding detailed walking and driving tours of the city area.

City Transportation
Alice Springs Airport is some 14 km (9 miles) south of the city center. Pay A$3.50 (A$5 return) for shuttle service up the Stuart Highway to downtown.

There's no public transportation in Alice Springs except for taxis, and they're rather expensive. If you want to get out and see the town, beyond what you can easily walk to, you have these options:

Rent a car for the day. You can get an open "moke" for as little as A$17 a day and 18 cents a km, plus $5 for insurance. (That's a cost of A$31 if you do 50 km of driving.) A compact will run A$25 a day and 18 cents a km.

Hire a car and driver, at a rate of A$35 for two hours. The Northern Territory Government Tourist Bureau has a list of operators.

Join a bus tour. Three-hour tours operated by Ansett, AAT King's and CATA Tours, among others, are priced at A$22, including all admissions.

Rent a bicycle or moped. Thrifty Bike Hire on Todd Street has bikes for A$6 an 8-hour day, mopeds for A$20 a day. The tourist bureau can tell you other locations.

Sightseeing Highlights
Anzac Hill, named in honor of the combined World War I and II armed forces of Australia and New Zealand, offers a good view of Alice Springs and the surrounding terrain. Drive the circular road off Stuart Highway, or hike the steep Lions Walk from the end of Bath Street off Wills Terrace.
▲▲**The Old Telegraph Station** is 3 km north of Alice Springs off the Stuart Highway. The reserve has restored the original 1972 telegraph station and equipment, and displays early photographs and historical documents. There are nature walks and a small wildlife park nearby, as well as a picnic ground and barbecue area beside the Alice Springs waterhole.
▲**The School of the Air** provides education by short-wave radio to children through the Central Australian Outback, some as far as 1,000 km (621 miles) away. Visitors are invited to observe and listen between 1:30 and 3:30 p.m. on school days (Monday to Friday except holidays). The school is located beside Braitling School in Head Street, about 1½ miles north of downtown.
▲▲**The Royal Flying Doctor Service** was established in 1939 by the Rev. John Flynn, probably The Alice's best-known historical figure, to deliver medical attention to isolated homesteads by small plane. Today it relies more on radio communication to serve thousands of square miles from New South Wales and Queensland to Western Australia. Tours of the base, near the south end of Bath Street on Stuart Terrace, are offered every half-hour from 9:00 to 11:30 a.m. and 2:00 to 3:30 p.m. Monday to Friday, and from 9:00 to 11:00 a.m. Saturday. Admission is A$1.50. (Flynn's original aircraft is on display at the Aviation Museum on Memorial Drive, at the old Alice Springs airport.)
▲**Panorama Guth,** 65 Hartley St. north of Stott Terrace, is the private gallery of painter Henk Guth, who has created an unusual 360-degree mural of the terrain surrounding Alice Springs. Guth also has a collection of photographs, Aboriginal artifacts and watercolor paintings of the Hermannsburg School. Open 9:00 a.m. to 5:00 p.m. Monday to Friday, 9:00 a.m. to noon and 2:00 to 5:00 p.m. Saturday, 2:00 to 5:00 p.m. Sunday. Admission is A$1.50.
▲**Pitchi Richi Sanctuary,** on Aranda Terrace south of Heavitree Gap near the Todd River causeway, combines William Ricketts' unique Aboriginal-theme sculpture with an outdoor folk museum and wild bird refuge. If you missed the Ricketts Sanctuary in the Dandenong Ranges east of Melbourne, don't miss this. Open daily 9:00 a.m. to sunset. Admission is A$1.50.
▲**Diarama Village,** 2 km west of downtown on Larapinta Drive at Bradshaw Drive, uses narrated dioramas to depict Aboriginal myths —like how the kangaroo got his tail and how

the Milky Way was formed. Open 10:00 a.m. to 5:00 p.m. daily; admission A$2.

▲Aboriginal art galleries exhibit and sell the arts and crafts of the native tribes of Central Australia—the Arunta, the Curindji and the Pitjantjatjara. Browse at the government-operated **Centre for Aboriginal Artists and Craftsmen**, 86 Todd St., or any of a dozen other shops and galleries.

Emily Gap Camel Farm, 4 km south of town on Emily Gap Road (the Ross Highway), is open for riding these "ships of the desert" from 8:00 a.m. to 5:00 p.m. daily. It also has a Magic Spark Museum of early radio communications. Admission is A$2.50.

The Mecca Date Garden on Emily Gap Road is Australia's only commercial date garden, with 20 varieties of productive date palms. Open daily 9:30 a.m. to 4:30 p.m. Admission, including a conducted tour, is A$1.50.

▲**The Henley-on-Todd Regatta** is perhaps the most exciting boating race never to talk place on water. Every year in the last weekend of August, 40-foot yachts line up in the dry river bed, gripped tightly on the gunwhale by their crews, who run with them as fast as they can. It's a good excuse for a party.

Where to Stay
The top of the line in Alice Springs is represented by the modern **Sheraton Alice Springs**, Barrett Drive (tel. 52-8000), followed closely by its next-door neighbor, **Lasseter's Casino** (tel. 52-5066). Both are on the south side of town. The **Elkira Motel**, 134 Bath St. (tel. 52-1411); the **Desert Rose Inn**, 15 Railway Terrace (tel. 52-1411); and the **Oasis Motel**, 10 Gap Road at Traeger Avenue (tel 52-1444), are centrally located and moderately priced.

For economy bracket lodging, try the **Arura Safari Lodge**, 18 Warburton St. at Lindsay Avenue (tel. 52-3843). The YWCA's **Stuart Lodge**, Stuart Terrace near Todd Street (tel. 52-1894), takes both men and women. Budget travelers can get a cheap bed at the **Sandrifter Safari Lodge**, 6 Kharlic St. (tel. 52-8686), or the **Alice Springs Youth Hostel** at the corner of Todd Street and Stott Terrace (tel. 52-5016).

Where to Eat
Aside from hotel coffee shops and restaurants, there is a good variety of dining establishments in Alice Springs. Steak and spicy food lovers appreciate **Overlanders Steakhouse**, 72 Hartley St., with meals in the A$8 to A$10 range. Ask for buffalo steak in witchety grub sauce. **The Todd Tavern**, at the corner of the Todd Street Mall and Wills Terrace, has several restaurants, including **The Other Place**, serving counter meals priced from A$4.50 and the more formal **Maxim's** for continental

cuisine. **Papa Luigi's Bistro**, at the north end of Todd Street, has pastas, steaks and chicken cacciatore for A$5 and up. **Chopsticks**, in the Ermond Arcade on Hartley Street, is the local Chinese favorite with Cantonese and Szechuan cuisine. Good, cheap breakfasts and lunches cost no more than A$5 at the Eranova Cafeteria, 72 Todd St.

Fifteen km (9 ½ miles) south of Alice Springs is **Chateau Hornsby**, Central Australia's first and only winery. The wine isn't great, but it's certainly palatable. . .and dry! There's an informal outdoor barbecue area, fine for lunches, and a pleasant indoor restaurant where local bush balladeer Ted Egan performs most nights. Find it at the end of Petrick Road, off Colonel Rose Drive.

On Sundays, Tuesdays and Fridays, for A$45, you can "Take a Camel to Dinner" by joining **Frontier Tours**' sundown safari down the Todd River bed to Chateau Hornsby. The price includes an hour on a camel's back and a five-course barramundi (fish) or buffalo roast dinner. The beasts leave Alice Springs at 4:00 p.m. (returning at 9:00 p.m.) October to April and depart at 3:00 p.m. May to September. Book at your hotel or call 53-0444.

Nightlife

Alice Springs isn't Sydney or Melbourne. But it does have a casino. **Lasseter's Casino** on Barrett Drive, on the southeast side of town, is named after Harold Lasseter, a local legend who perished in the desert searching for a fabled reef of gold in 1931. Harry should have lived so long; the gold is here, on the gaming tables. The casino also has a disco open Thursday 11:00 p.m. to 4:00 a.m., Friday and Saturday 11:00 p.m. to 5:00 a.m.

There's live music Thursday to Sunday at the **Todd Tavern**, Wills Terrace and Todd Street Mall, and the **Stuart Arms Hotel**, Parsons Street and Todd Street Mall. **Bojangles Nightclub**, Todd Street near Stott Terrace is open nightly except Sunday for meals and Disco dancing 'til the wee hours.

If there's more upscale entertainment in town, you'll find it at the **Araluen Arts Centre**, west of downtown on Larapinta Drive. The Alice's center for the performing and visual arts attracts name entertainers from Australia and overseas.

DAY 12
ALICE SPRINGS TO AYERS ROCK

Marvel at the weird geology of the Red Centre as you fly from Alice
Springs to Yulara resort village at Ayers Rock, arriving in the early
afternoon. After getting settled in your lodging and exploring
the community, join the sunset barbecue tour to The Olgas.

Suggested Schedule	
9:00	You'll have time to do some shopping or sightseeing in Alice Springs before taking a shuttle bus to the airport.
11:35	Ansett N.T. Flight BT278 for Ayers Rock.
12:20	Arrive at Ayers Rock's Connellan Airport.
1:00	Get settled in your accommodations, take a dip in the pool, then drop by the Yulara Visitors Centre and tour the resort complex.
4:30	Depart on "Outback" barbecue-tour to the Olgas.
9:30	Return to hotel.

Ayers Rock Orientation
The great red monolith of Ayers Rock is the symbol of Australian Outback, at once irresistable spiritual force to the Aboriginal people and a testimony to the stark primeval beauty of the
desert landscape.

There is no larger rock on earth. Yet Ayers Rock may not be as
well as known for its massive size (1,260 feet high, 5½ miles
around its base) as for its moods. From dawn to dusk, the Rock
undergoes a continuous series of subtle color changes, from
sunrise pink to midday brown, sunset red to post-sunset purple. During the rare desert downpours, it can even appear
silvery with rain cascading down its time-sculpted slopes.

The ancient Loritja and Pitjantjatjara tribes called the Rock
"Uluru." Thousands of years ago, they decorated the cave walls
around its base with paintings and petroglyphs. Not until 1872
did Europeans know of the Rock; Ernest Giles sighted it during
his explorations of the Centre, and the following year, William
Gosse led a three-month camel caravan to climb the monolith.
Today, the ascent is a relatively simple, if strenuous, morning
excursion.

About 510 square miles surrounding Ayers Rock and the nearby
Olgas range, piled high like a giant's marbles above the sandy
earth, were established in 1958 as Ayers Rock-Mount Olga Na-

tional Park. Title for the parklands was transferred to the Aboriginal people in 1985, and Uluru National Park came into being. Commercial enterprise—motels, a campground and an airstrip—was moved out of the shadow of the Rock at that time. A new resort village, Yulara, was created outside the northern boundary of the park, 19 km (12 miles) from the Rock.

Yulara was built to provide comfort in the desert sun for the rapidly growing influx of tourists. Only 2,300 people visited Ayers Rock when the national park first opened in 1958; but by 1987, with a sealed, 468 km (291 miles) all-weather road linking the Rock to Alice Springs, Uluru was attracting 220,000 visitors from all over the world—despite being one of the costliest destinations in Australia.

The resort village, completed in 1984, can accommodate up to 5,000 people a day in two luxury hotels, a mid-priced lodge and a spacious campground. And it is a complete village—in fact, with its resident population of around 500, it is the third largest community in the sparsely settled Northern Territory (after Darwin and Alice Springs). There's a small shopping square, a school, a medical center, a community hall and sports center, a police station, and other facilities to keep the people from feeling too isolated.

Still, they must cope with the summer heat and year-round temperature extremes. From December to February, daytime temperatures average about 97 degrees Fahrenheit, dropping to around 70 at night; mid-winter temperatures range from average daytime highs of 58 to nightime lows of 41, though freezing temperatures are not uncommon. Total rainfall is only 10 inches a year, with February the wettest month (1½ inches) and September the driest (¼ inch).

Yulara Transportation

There isn't any cheap way to get around here, short of walking. The shuttle bus for the short hop from the airport to Yulara costs A$5 one way; the price of the three-times-a-day shuttle from the resort to Ayers Rock is A$12 return, or about 50 cents a mile. And so it goes. The Ayers Rock Touring Co. has the concession. Some visitors find the three-day "Rock Pass," allowing unlimited trips on the shuttle buses to the Rock and the Olgas, a worthwhile purchase at A$39.

Cars are available for rent, but they're hardly a bargain. If the weather cooperates—and it usually does—consider hiring a moped from the Mobil Service Station in Yulara village. Half-day (four-hour) rental is 20, full-day A$30.

Where to Stay

The **Sheraton Ayers Rock Hotel** (tel. 56-2200) is the luxury leader, with 230 rooms rambling around a lovely swimming pool and courtyard. Twin rooms are A$135 a night. Many visitors prefer the A$120 rooms across the village at the **Four Seasons Ayers Rock Motel** (tel. 56-2100). From these two inns, it's an abrupt step down-market to the **Ayers Rock Lodge** (tel. 56-2170), offering bare-bones family units or cabins for four at A$48, hostel-style dorm accommodations at A$12 a bunk.

Where to Eat

The **Sheraton** has two fine restaurants, the **Four Seasons** another. At either hotel, you can get a filling buffet dinner for around A$25. There are three less expensive options, perhaps the best being the counter meals and buffet at the **Ernest Giles Tavern**, open daily in the Shopping Square. The adjacent **Old Oak Tree Coffee Shop** has light meals and takeaways, while the **Ayers Rock Lodge Food Bar** is popular for its casual home cooking.

Today's Sightseeing Highlight

▲▲**The Olgas**, to many visitors, are even more spectacular than Ayers Rock itself. An accumulation of 36 oddly shaped domes that rise from the Central Australian desert some 32 km (20 miles) west of the Rock, they were known to the Aboriginals as Katajuta and feared as hungry giants. Indeed, the Olgas can be sirens who lure explorers into their seductive wonderland only to cook them alive in a midday oven. As recently as 1987, foreign visitors died in the Olgas on two separate occasions.

By late afternoon, the heat is off again. One way to appreciate these geological curiosities is with the Ayers Rock Touring Company's "Evening in the Outback" tour. You'll be picked up in Yulara about 4:30 p.m., head out to the west side of the Olgas to watch the colorful sunset, then drive to an isolated spot for a "steak-and-snags" barbecue under the Southern Cross. If you shine a flashlight toward the darkness around your campfire, you may see the shining eyes of wild dingoes waiting to feast on your leftovers. The tour's major drawback is its price—A$39, not acceptable on the Rock Pass. (Hours are a half-hour later for mid-October through March.)

Nightlife

A bush band performs Aussie sing-along and dance music most nights in the Sheraton's **Mulgara Bar**. It's good fun, the best reason to visit the Sheraton if you're not staying there. The **Ernest Giles Tavern** has a pub disco several nights of the week.

DAY 13
AYERS ROCK

Learn about the Aboriginal culture today. Spend the morning
with a native guide who will show you how his people found
food, water, shelter and medicine in this arid landscape. Visit
the craft exhibit at the Uluru National Park ranger station and
search for ancient petroglyphs in caves around the base of Ayers
Rock. Back at Yulara, sip champagne as you watch the sun set
over the red rock.

Suggested Schedule

7:00	Leave Yulara via shuttle bus for Ayers Rock.
7:30	While others are beginning their ascent, stroll to Maggie Springs, then to the ranger station.
8:30	"Liru" walk with Aboriginal guide.
10:45	Return to the ranger station to see the outdoor exhibit of Aboriginal crafts and video.
12:15	Back to Yulara aboard shuttle bus.
1:00	Lunch, swim, relax.
Open	Go to the Sheraton lookout tower 45 minutes before sunset to sip champagne and watch the Rock's colors change. Then dinner.
9:00	Early bedtime for tomorrow's "ordeal."

Sightseeing Highlights
▲▲**Maggie Springs**, known to the Pitjantjatjara as Mutitjulu, is
a deep, tranquil pool nestled against the southeast wall of Ayers
Rock. After a rainstorm, you can often see tiny desert frogs and
fairy shrimp in the water. The hideaway is especially striking in
the late morning, when the blue of the Outback sky contrasts
sharply with the red of the rock and the green of the mulga and
desert oak vegetation. Nearby are several small caves, their walls
and roofs adorned with Aboriginal cave paintings thousands of
years old. Maggie Springs are a level 2½ km walk from the shuttle bus stop.
  ▲▲**The Liru Walk** only happens twice a week, but it's worth
catching when it does. Beginning at 8:30 a.m. Tuesdays and
Thursdays, an Aboriginal woman (females are the traditional
food-gatherers in Central Australia) leads a group from the
Uluru National Park Ranger Station on a two-hour bush walk to
demonstrate how her people survived in this arid climate using
only natural food sources. You'll learn, for instance, that the
burrowing witchety grub is superb food, 50% protein and 50%

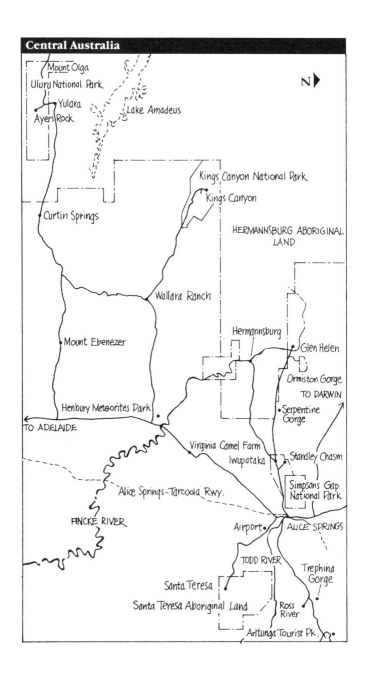

Central Australia

Mount Olga
Uluru National Park
Yulara
Ayers Rock
Lake Amadeus
N ▶

Kings Canyon National Park
Kings Canyon

Curtin Springs

HERMANNSBURG ABORIGINAL
LAND

Wallara Ranch

Hermannsburg
Glen Helen

Mount Ebenezer
Ormiston Gorge

TO DARWIN

Henbury Meteorites Park
Serpentine
Gorge

TO ADELAIDE

Virginia Camel Farm
Standley Chasm
Iwupataka

Alice Springs-Tarcoola Rwy.
Simpsons Gap
National Park

FINCKE RIVER
Airport
ALICE SPRINGS

Trephina
Gorge
TODD RIVER

Santa Teresa
Santa Teresa Aboriginal Land
Ross
River
Arltunga Tourist Pk.

fat, that the fruit of the plumbush tree has the highest known concentration of Vitamin C; that the prolific mulga tree has seeds that can be ground to make flour; and that the flowers of the hakea tree, mixed with water, make a drink similar to cola. And remember that scene in "Crocodile Dundee" where Mick skewers a large lizard for dinner? Your guide will show you where to find a tasty sand goanna just like it.

In fact, there is a bewildering variety of wildlife here in the desert. Naturalists have counted 290 species of plant life, 151 birds, 52 reptiles and 22 native mammals. The most prolific of all creatures is the blowfly, sort of a larger, more persistent version of the American housefly. Without direct sunlight, and with a bit of a breeze, they're not bad. In most circumstances, they're extremely unpleasant. You'll soon learn why "The Great Australian Salute" is a hand waving past your face to keep these flies out of your eyes, nose, ears and mouth.

Flies notwithstanding, the Liru Walk is a fascinating look at a lifestyle very different from our own. Tour numbers are limited, so book ahead by phoning 56-2988. The tour concludes at the base of the Rock climb, leaving a 20-minute return walk to the ranger station.

▲**Uluru National Park Ranger Station,** where everyone who enters the park is supposed to stop and pay a A$1.50 use fee, has a number of exhibits of special interest to the park visitor. In particular, take some time to talk with the Aboriginal people displaying local, hand-made arts and crafts in a special outdoor area.

DAY 14
AYERS ROCK TO WALLARA RANCH

If the world's largest monolith is awesome at sunset, it's even
more stunning at dawn. Awaken early to watch the spectacle,
and to beat the heat and flies as you scale the huge Red Rock.
Then you too can wear a T-shirt declaring: "I Climbed Ayers
Rock." After lunch, board a bus for the 125-mile drive to Wallara
Ranch, where you'll spend the night at an Outback station.

Suggested Schedule	
6:45	Leave Yulara via shuttle bus for Ayers Rock.
7:30	Begin climb up Ayers Rock. Allow 90 minutes for the return trip.
9:00	Tour base of Rock by bus, or preferable, with ranger guide to Kantju Gorge.
11:45	Return to Yulara via shuttle bus. Lunch.
1:30	Farewell to Ayers Rock.
3:30	Rest stop at Angas Downs turnoff.
5:30	Arrive Wallara Ranch for overnight stay.

Sightseeing Highlights
▲▲▲**Climbing Ayers Rock** is a must, as long as you're in
reasonably good physical condition. The ever-cautious national park administration warns that the average time of climbing the 1.6 km (1 mile) to the cairn and returning to the foot of
the Rock is two hours. As a slightly out-of-shape, over-the-hill
hiker, I can accomplish it in a little over an hour, including 15
minutes or so relaxing and taking photos at the top. But don't
push yourself too hard; if you feel exhausted or nauseous, quit.
Take a break, then head back down.

The first 500 meters of the climb are the steepest. A staunch
chain has been sunk into the Rock to provide a handhold for
any and all who need it while ascending the 45 to 60-degree
angle. Once that portion has been surmounted, it's merely an
uphill walk, with just a couple of precipitous drops and rises
across eroded ridges.

At the top, you'll be rewarded with an unfettered view of
hundreds of miles of red dirt. Be sure to sign the climbers'
register, noting the vast array of nationalities who have put their
home address there next to your own. After a short rest, you
can head back down. Your calves got a workout on the way up;
now your thighs will feel it. Some climbers find it easier to back
down the chain on the steepest stretch.

The best shoes for climbing are rubber-soled. Any kind of athletic shoes work as well as proper climbing boots. Don't go in street shoes, thongs or bare feet. Bring something with you to drink, and if you're starting much later than 8:00 a.m., put on suntan lotion and a sun hat. The wind can be stiff on the rock, so be sure to tie down anything you carry—or it may wind up at the bottom of the Rock long before you do.

▲**Circling the Rock** aboard the shuttle bus can be done if you're back at the base by 9:00 a.m. The driver-guide points out Taputji (Little Ayers Rock), Maggie Springs and other sites around the Rock's circumference en route back to Yulara. It's interesting to note how different Ayers Rock appears from different aspects. The tour costs A$15, including the A$12 shuttle free from Yulara.

▲**Ranger-guided walks**, which also leave at 9:00 a.m. from the car park at the base of the Rock climb, are free. For over an hour, hikers accompany a park ranger into Kantju Gorge, a cleft in the Rock with an adjacent waterhole. The ranger explains Ayers Rock's place in Aboriginal legend, and tells about the geology and environment of this Central Australian region.

▲▲**Ayers Rock-Kings Canyon tours** are conducted by several tour companies based in Alice Springs. Any Northern Territory Government Tourist Bureau can provide a complete listing. I like the low-budget tour offered by A-01/Spinifex Tours (write Fan Arcade, Todd Street Mall, Alice Springs, NT 5750, tel., 089/52-5424 or 52-2203). But its tours are Saturday-to-Monday and Tuesday-to-Thursday expeditions, not helpful to those of us leaving Yulara on a Friday. My second choice is Ansett Trailways (Todd and Parsons Streets, Alice Springs, NT 5750, tel. 089/52-2422), which has daily departures on the three-day Alice-Ayers Rock-Kings Canyon-Alice circuit. The trick is to join a tour in progress on departure from Yulara. Advance arrangements are essential.

You'll leave Yulara on the Lasseter Highway, a 247 km (153 mile) thoroughfare connecting Ayers Rock with the Stuart Highway, the main north-south route from Adelaide to Darwin. About 138 km (86 miles) from Yulara, following a rest stop at the Curtin Springs homestead and a view of isolated Mount Connor, you'll turn north past Angas Downs to the Wallara Ranch, 70 km (43 miles) further.

Wallara Ranch offers bunkhouse and private, four-to-a-room cabin accommodations for economy prices. There's also a dining room with filling, country-style meals.

DAY 15
WALLARA RANCH TO ALICE SPRINGS

Scramble through the sheer walls of colorful Kings Canyon, then return to Alice Springs in the evening. If you're not totally exhausted, enjoy a nightcap at the casino.

Suggested Schedule

6:00	Rise and shine; eat breakfast.
7:00	Leave for Kings Canyon.
9:00	Explore the spactacular chasm. Wander through the lush Garden of Eden and climb to the canyon rim for marvelous panoramic views.
11:30	Leave Kings Canyon.
1:30	Lunch at Wallara Ranch.
3:00	Leave for Alice Springs.
5:00	See the Henbury Craters.
6:30	Arrive at Alice Springs for the night.

Sightseeing Highlights
▲▲▲**Kings Canyon**—Australia's spectacular "Grand Canyon" is a deep cleft in the George Gill Ranges, about 250 km—155 air miles—southwest of Alice Springs. (From the Wallara Ranch it's a 99-km, or 61-mile, drive each way.)

Sheer sandstone walls rising 700 to 900 feet above the canyon floor vary in hue from pink to crimson, ivory to deep purple. In the Garden of Eden, lush palms grow around dozens of waterholes, reflecting the multi-colored walls like so many kaleidoscopes. In the Lost City, rocky outcrops look like primitive rock dwellings of a forgotten tribe. The Sphinx is another formation unique in this terrain. You may find rock wallabies and goanna lizards at the waterholds, and you'll certainly see rose-tinted galahs and a variety of other birds.

It's a steep climb to the canyon rim—more difficult than the struggle up Ayers Rock—but the panoramic views from the summit make the climb worthwhile. As at the Rock, you should wear rubber-soled shoes for climbing, apply suntan lotion, wear a sun hat, and carry something to drink.

Kings Canyon Road runs the 198 km (123 miles) from the canyon to the Stuart Highway, via the midway stop at Wallara Ranch. This is a graded-dirt road, typical of the Outback. Tour bus drivers who ply this route regularly have taken all appropriate precautions for Outback travel, but if you're driving yourself, you should follow the old Boy Scout axiom and "Be Prepared."

Watch out for road flooding, particularly where it crosses the Palmer River. This arid land doesn't absorb rainfall quickly, so even a half-inch of precipitation can have a major effect on road conditions. Beware of collisions with kangaroos, wild camels and brumbies (wild horses). Carry water—at least a gallon per person per day of your trip—plus reserve gas, a tool kit, two spare tires and extra engine parts. It helps if you have a mechanical inclination.

▲**Henbury Craters** are an odd cluster of about a dozen meteor craters off Kings Canyon Road near its junction with the Stuart Highway, 132 km (82 miles) south of Alice Springs. Between 2,000 and 3,000 years ago, a shower of meteorites rained down upon this 40-acre conservation park, creating craters from 20 to 600 feet across and as much as 50 feet deep. A walking trail from the car park signposts many of the features.

▲**The Virginia Camel Farm**, 90 km (56 miles) south of the Alice, is Noel Fullerton's contribution to Central Australian culture. Fullerton originated Alice Springs' Lions Club ''Camel Cup'' in the 1970s, won it himself four times, and now has placed his teen-age children in the championship category of camel-riding. (The Cup races are held annually in May.) The farm domesticates some of the Center's estimated 15,000 wild camels and breeds others for export to—of all places—the Arab world, from which Australia's herd originated! Visitors can pay a few dollars for a short camel ride, or book a one or two-week safari east into the Rainbow Valley.

DAY 16
ALICE SPRINGS TO CAIRNS

Today, fly from Alice Springs to Cairns. On arrival in Cairns, the
humidity will tell you immediately that you're in the tropics.
Have a cold beer at an Esplanade pub, watch the fishing and
pleasure boats return from the Great Barrier Reef, see the Reef
World aquarium. For dinner, order barramundi, a delectable
river-run cod.

Suggested Schedule	
8:30	Leisurely breakfast at hotel, then take a shuttle bus to the airport.
10:55	Ansett Flight #285 to Cairns.
1:20	Arrive at Cairns International Airport. Take a shuttle bus 8 km to town and check into hotel.
3:00	Stroll down the Esplanade and around town. See the Reef World aquarium, the marlin jetty, and perhaps the museum or House of 10,000 Shells.
6:30	Dinner at one of Cairn's fine seafood eateries.

Cairns Orientation
Cairns (don't pronounce the "r") is the undeclared capital of
lazy, tropical North Queensland. A rapidly growing town of
about 70,000 people on the shores of Trinity Bay, it is wedged
against a backdrop of rainforest-clad mountains, facing the so-
called eighth wonder of the world, the Great Barrier Reef.

Founded in the mid-1870s as a customs collection point and
a port for gold and tin mines in the interior of Queensland, it
later grew as a center for sugar-cane growing and processing.
Sugar and tin remain economically important today, along with
fishing, timber and tropical fruit.

But tourism is taking over as the No. 1 revenue producer. From
1979 to 1984 the number of tourists coming to this lush location
more than doubled, and there are indications that the number
could redouble by 1990. Thirteen new hotels with over 2,600
rooms were built in the greater Cairns area between 1985 and
1987, and another five hotels with about 1,000 rooms were scheduled to open in 1988. The Cairns airport now has direct flight
connections with nearby Papua New Guinea and with the U.S.
West Coast, making it more accessible to tourists than ever before.

Why do the tourists come? The primary reason is the Reef.
No population center along the Australian coast is closer to the
coral phenomenon than Cairns, with Green Island a mere

40-minute launch trip away. Second, they come for the fishing.
Cairns is famed for it sportfishing fleet; international personal-
ities such as actor Lee Marvin use Cairns as a base for marlin
fishing. Third, they come for the jungle. Some of the last great
tracts of rainforest on Earth are west of Cairns, on the Atherton
Tableland, and north, around Cape Tribulation.

Cairns itself is an easy town to find your way around. It's
stereotypically tropical, its ornate wide-verandaed homes often
raised well above the ground for air circulation. The streets are
wide and palm-fringed, the harbor a bustling center of trade
amid squawking sea birds. Spence Street runs due west from
the marlin jetty; it's paralleled to the north by Shields, Aplin,
Florence, Minnie and Upward Streets. The Esplanade, which
runs along the shore from Upward to Spence, and McLeod
Street, which fronts the railroad tracks, mark the eastern and
western boundaries of the downtown district. Abbot, Lake,
Grafton and Sheridan Streets run between, from east to west.
City Place, a mall marking the center of the city, is at the in-
tersecton of Shields and Lake. Sheridan Street is the main
thoroughfare north toward the airport and the Cook Highway.

City Transportation
A regular shuttle-bus service operates between Cairns International Airport and town, a distance of 8 km (5 miles), for A$3.
(Leaving town, call 53-4722 for pickup times.) Taxi fare between Cairns and the airport is about A$7.

If you arrived in Cairns by train from Brisbane or other points
south, you'll disembark at Cairns Station on McLeod Street, at

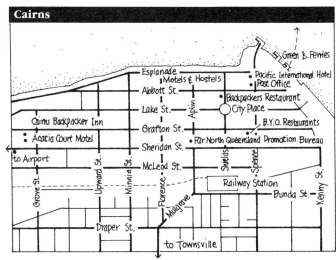

the end of Shields St. All downtown points are within easy walking distance. (The economy single adult rail fare from Brisbane to Cairns, one-way, is A$84.80. Trains arrive Tuesday through Friday plus Sunday at 7:45 p.m.; the Queenslander express comes in Monday only at 5:55 p.m.)

A variety of bus services are available within and around Cairns at reasonable fares. (Schedules are posted in the foyer of the O.T. Corporation and on the window of Rockman's, both on Shield Street between City Place and Abbott Street.) There are interstate bus terminals for Greyhound at 78 Grafton St. and Ansett Pioneer at 58 Shields St.

Car rentals are also readily available in town and at the airport. For cheap moke or moped rentals, check with Mini Car Rental, 143 Sheridan St. You can rent bicycles in several locations, including Cycle Works, Aplin and Lake Streets, and the Bicycle Barn, 61 Sheridan St.

Where to Stay
With all those new hotels, and some three dozen others, there's a wide variety of accommodation available in Cairns. Generally speaking, you'll find the budget and moderate lodging in the town itself. Luxury hotels are often up the coast, the best currently being the **Ramada Reef Resort** at Palm Cove (tel. 070/55-3999), about 25 km (16 miles) north of Cairns. It will be dwarfed when Sheraton's A$150 million **Four Mile Beach Resort**, 76 km (47 miles) from Cairns at Port Douglas, opens in late 1987 with an 18-hole championship golf course and hovercraft connection to Cairns International Airport.

The No. 1 hotel in Cairns is the **Pacific International Hotel**, 43 The Esplanade (tel. 070/51-7888), with three restaurants, three bars and a health club. Its preeminence will soon be challenged by a new Hilton and a new Park Royal.

In the moderate price class, it would be hard to do better than the **Cairns Colonial Club**, 18-26 Cannon St. (tel. 53-5111), which surmounts the minor drawback of being a couple miles north of the city centre with regular free shuttle service. A choice of rooms at several price levels starting at A$49 are nestled around an open-air restaurant-bar and saltwater pool, complete with sandy beach and waterfall.

Economy travelers will do well at the **Silver Palms Private Hotel**, 153 The Esplanade (tel. 51-2059), and the **Linga Longa**, 223 The Esplanade (tel. 51-3013), both equipped with kitchens. And those touring on a shoestring will quickly learn why Cairns is becoming one of the budget travel capitals of the world. The biggest of five hostels is **Caravella's**, 77-81 The Esplanade (tel. 51-2159). A bit quieter is the **Cairns Backpackers Inn**, 255 Lake St. (tel. 51-9166).

Sightseeing Highlights

Once you're settled, it's time to see the sights of town. Cairns is better known as a base for excursions to the Reef and inland, but these will fill an afternoon.

▲▲**The Marlin Jetty** is a "must" stop during the sportfishing season, which runs from August into December. When private boats and charter operators return here toward evening with their days' catches, the heart of even the veteran fisherman has to thump a little. Black marlin, hoisted onto the scales, may go well over the 1,000 pound mark.

▲**Reef World** is an aquarium on Marlin Parade with a variety of saltwater species—crocodiles, turtles, sharks, giant clams, and a great many fish, including barramundi, huge groupers and the poisonous stonefish. There's even a stingray who is fed by hand every day at 9:00 p.m. Open daily from 10:00 a.m. to 5:30 p.m.; admission is A$3.

▲**Windows on the Reef**, located off Wharf Street on the Great Barrier Reef cruise docks, simulates a night dive on the reef from within a small rotating theatre. The 45-minute show is a good introduction to the massive coral creation not far off shore. Open daily 10:00 a.m. to 5:30 p.m. Admission is A$4.

▲**The Cairns Museum**, located in an early 20th Century School of Arts building at the corner of Lake and Shields streets, has displays of natural history, North Queensland Aboriginal artifacts, gold-mining (and early Chinese habitation) and railway construction. Open 10:00 a.m. to 3:00 p.m. Monday to Friday. Admission is A$1.

Cairns Botanical Gardens, Collins Avenue in Edge Hill, two miles from the town center, comprise a luxuriant century-old tropical jungle and parkland with more than 10,000 species of trees, shrubs and flowers. There's a great view across Cairns to Trinity Bay from the top of Mount Whitfield. Open daily sunrise to sunset. Admission is free.

Where to Eat

For a relatively small city, Cairns offers an awesome variety of international cuisine in its many restaurants.

Some of the licensed seafood restaurants have the most style. Try **Scuppers**, Grafton and Aplin Streets; **Fathoms**, Grove and Diggers Streets (near Grafton), especially for the garlic chili crab; or **Tawny's** on the Marlin Jetty. **Lin Nam**, 14 Aplin St., has good Chinese seafood. An excellent BYO seafood eatery is **Avocado**, 228 Sheridan St.

Among other BYO restaurants, these are a few of the best, by cuisine: **Der Feinschmecker** (German), 95 Grafton St.; **Thuggee Bill's** (Indian), 42 Aplin St.; **Toto Baru** (Indonesian), 42 Spence St.; **Omar Khayyam** (Lebanese), 82 Sheridan St., **Rah-**

mah's (Malaysian), 47 Shields St.; **Little Gringo** (Mexican), 95 Grafton St.; **Casa Gomez** (Spanish), 48 Aplin St.; **Sweethearts** (vegetarian), Rusty's Bar on Grafton Street.

Along the Esplanade and around the City Place mall, several restaurants have outdoor tables set up to catch the eyes and noses of passers-by. One of the most popular for lunch is **Swagman's Rest**, City Place.

Last, but far from least, is the **Backpackers' Restaurant** on Shields Street just east of City Place. With a name like that, its clientele is—you guessed it—mainly backpackers. And it's always packed. Counter meals are cheap and good, beer is cheap and good, and both are served into the wee hours.

Nightlife

The scene changes often in a resort town like Cairns, but at this writing, the favored upscale nightclubs were the **Playpen International**, 2 Lake St.; **Scandals**, in the Tradewinds Sunlodge at Lake and Florence streets; and the **House on the Hill**, Kingsford Street in out-of-the-way Mooroobool. All are open until 3 in the morning, also nights of closing vary.

Close to the city center, and more in the vein of a quiet drink and conversation to a piano bar or light jazz, are **The Nest**, 82 McLeod St.; **Duke's**, upstairs at 86 Lake St.; and **Kipling's Wine Bar**, 79 Abbott St.

Young rockers find loud music and cheap drinks at the **Hideaway Tavern**, Lake Street between Spence and Shield. **Hides Hotel**, at the southwest corner of City Place, is always good for a rage. You'll often find the fishermen in the **Marlin Bar** at the Great Northern Hotel, 69 Abbott St.

You might also get a kick out of **Milliway's**, an upstairs BYO built around the theme of Douglas Adams' spacey novel, *A Hitchhikers' Guide to the Galaxy*. this BYO cafe upstairs at 144 Graton St. offers a place where any traveling musician can drop by to jam for all he (or she) is worth.

Helpful Hints

The two best sources of travel and touring information once you've arrived in Cairns are the Far North Queensland Promotion Bureau, corner of Sheridan and Aplin Streets (tel. 51-3588), and the Queensland Government Travel Centre, 12 Shields St. (tel. 51-4066). Both are open weekdays 9:00 a.m. to 5:00 p.m.

The General Post Office is on the corner of Florence and Sheridan Streets. Banks stay open from 9:30 a.m. to 4:00 p.m. Monday to Thursday, to 5:00 p.m. Friday. Retail shops in the downtown area open 8:30 a.m. to 5:15 p.m. Monday to Thursday, to 9:00 p.m. Friday, to noon Saturday.

In case of emergencies, dial 000.

DAY 17
GREEN ISLAND

Ship out for Green Island, a tiny coral cay 40 minutes' cruise
offshore where you can swim, study sea life from a glass-
bottom boat, view the world's largest crocodile in captivity,
and dine, drink and sleep at the small resort.

Suggested Schedule

7:00	Breakfast at hotel. Stow whatever bags you won't need on the island to await your return tomorrow night.
8:30	Leave for Green Island aboard Hayles' Cruises 220-passenger catamaran.
11:00	Walk around the island. It takes 20 minutes.
12:00	Lay on the beach some more.
1:00	Lunch, if you're ready.
2:30	Siesta.
3:30	Snorkeling again, or visit the croc.
6:00	Happy hour.
7:00	Dinner.

Alternative Schedule for Budget Travelers

9:00	Leave for Fitzroy Island aboard the MV Fitzroy catamaran.
9:45	Arrive at Fitzroy Island. Snorkel over the coral or go bushwalking in the rainforest.
1:00	Lunch. Rest of day on the beach at Fitzroy.

Sightseeing Highlights
▲▲▲**Green Island** is a misnomer. It's green, all right, cloaked
in lush palms, figs and other rainforest vegetation, but at a mere
32 acres in size, and nowhere more than 10 feet in elevation, it's
hardly classifiable as an island! In fact, you can walk around this
isolated coral cay, 17 miles offshore from Cairns, in about 20
minutes.

But Green Island's miniature size is part of its charm. Most of
the islet is reserved as a marine national park for its fine plant
and bird life. It's completely fringed by a beach of fine white
sand, and the offshore snorkeling is excellent.

Hayles' Cruises (tel. 51-5644) operate a transit service from
the Green Island Jetty off Wharf Street opposite Abbott Street.
Luxury catamarans—double-deckers complete with bars—
leave at 8:30 and 10:30 a.m. daily on the 40-minute journey.

The adult fare is A$23 return. Ordinary launches leave at 9:00 a.m. daily, making the trip in 90 minutes for A$12 return.

Once on the island, what's there to do? Well, to begin with, there's that fabulous beach. Swim, snorkel, skin dive, even try windsurfing. (Equipment is available for rent at reasonable rates on the beach.) You can try casting a line for reef fish, or just communing with nature in the forest.

At the end of the boat jetty, anchored on the seabed, is the **Green Island Underwater Observatory**, where you can descend to the ocean floor to gaze through large viewing windows at luminescent tropical fish flitting through colorful banks of coral, itself inhabited by starfish, anemones, giant clams and other undersea creatures. Admission is A$3.20.

On shore, **Marineland Melanesia** is an indoor-outdoor aquarium combined with a New Guinean artifact collection. It's worth visiting mainly to see its crocodiles. Well over a dozen of the ill-tempered reptiles are in residence here, including one Guiness-class monster nearly 20 feet long. He usually hides under his lily pads, but one glimpse of his huge jaws thrashing after a chunk of raw meat at feeding time will remind you why you should never go swimming alone in a saltwater estuary. Admission is A$3.50. Next door to this Marineland is the **Castaway Theatre**, which offers an underwater camera's perspective of the wonders of the Great Barrier Reef.

The comfortable **Green Island Reef Resort** has private lodging for A$54 to A$69 a night ($10 more in the mid-summer holiday season). The price includes dinner (usually a choice of meat or a reef fish) and a buffet breakfast. Lunch at the outdoor grill and drinks in the lounge are extra.

▲▲**Fitzroy Island**—Fitzroy is a much larger island than Green—about 750 acres—but a much smaller resort. That makes it ideal for travelers seeking a bit of isolation.

Located 3½ miles off the coast 16 miles east of Cairns, this mountainous island is shrouded in tropical rainforest and fringed by rugged coral beaches. It's not great for sunbathing, but there's an excellent reef 150 feet offshore for snorkeling and diving. You can rent equipment for those sports as well as canoeing and paddle skiing. Or you can go off on your own long bushwalks through the dense vegetation.

The *MV Fitzroy* catamaran (A$11 return) leaves Cairns daily at 9:00 a.m., reaching Fitzroy at 9:45 p.m. It departs Fitzroy at 1:30 p.m. for passage back to Cairns via Green Island.

The **Fitzroy Island Resort** on Welcome Bay caters to budget travelers with hostel-style rooms (A$25 for two) with communal kitchens. It also has guest villas for $79 full board ($90 single). The licensed dining room specializes in seafood.

DAY 18
GREAT BARRIER REEF

You'll leave Green Island this morning to spend the day snorkeling or diving on the outer Barrier Reef. It is an incredible experience to see more than 200 species of tropical reef fish swimming through an undersea "garden" of multicolored coral. Return to Cairns at night.

Suggested Schedule

11:15	Leave Green Island aboard Hayles' Reef Cat for Michaelmas Cay and Hastings Reef.
12:15	Arrive at Hastings Reef.
3:15	Leave Hastings Reef.
5:15	Return to Cairns after 15-minute pick-up and drop-off stop at Green Island.
5:30	Get re-established at hotel.
6:30	Dinner, perhaps followed by tropical nightlife.

Alternative Schedule (for Fitzroy Island overnighters)

1:30	Depart Fitzroy Island.
2:00	Arrive Green Island.
4:30	Leave Green Island.
5:15	Return to Cairns. Remainder of day as above.

Sightseeing Highlights
▲▲▲**The Great Barrier Reef** is truly one of the wonders of the world. Stretching for more than 2,000 km (1,250 miles) down the coast of Queensland from New Guinea to the Tropic of Capricorn, it is the largest structure (80,000 square miles of individual reefs, shoals and islets) ever created by living creatures.

Tiny marine animals called polyps (closely related to sea anemones) are the master engineers. Forming colonies linked by a network of tubes and protected by an external skeleton of lime, they forever grow upon the mass remains of their forebears. Their formations are as varied in color as in shape, from red fans to yellow staghorn, purple "brains" to green cabbage, and many, many more.

Snorkeling or diving in the Reef is like taking a swim through an underwater garden. I've put on a mask and fins in bodies of water all over the world, from Hawaii to the Indian Ocean, but never have I been more astounded than on the Barrier Reef. More than 1,400 species of fish have been identified here, each

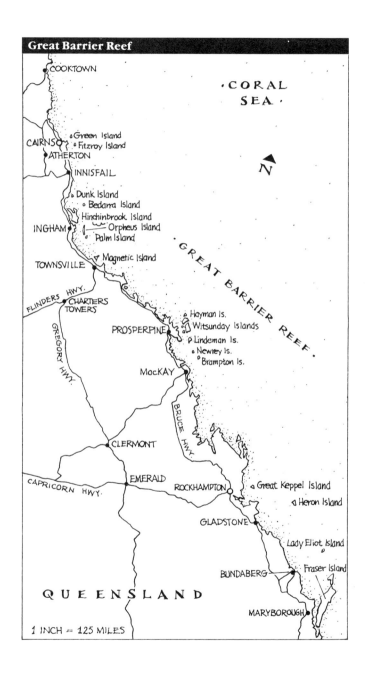

Great Barrier Reef

COOKTOWN

· C O R A L
S E A ·

Green Island
Fitzroy Island
CAIRNS
ATHERTON

INNISFAIL

Dunk Island
Bedarra Island
Hinchinbrook Island
INGHAM — Orpheus Island
Palm Island

Magnetic Island
TOWNSVILLE

G R E A T   B A R R I E R   R E E F

FLINDERS HWY.
CHARTERS TOWERS

GREGORY HWY.

Hayman Is.
Witsunday Islands
PROSPERPINE
Lindeman Is.
Newrey Is.
Brampton Is.

MacKAY

BRUCE HWY.

CLERMONT

CAPRICORN HWY.
EMERALD
ROCKHAMPTON
Great Keppel Island
Heron Island
GLADSTONE

Lady Eliot Island

BUNDABERG
Fraser Island

Q U E E N S L A N D

MARYBOROUGH

1 INCH = 125 MILES

seemingly brighter and more fanciful than the next. There are turtles and rays, starfish and sea urchins, jellyfish and giant clams, and more.

The polyps' only known enemy, by the way—besides the polluting or vandalizing human—is the crown-of-thorns star-fish. This creature is a formidable foe indeed, one posing a real challenge to marine biologists trying to control the escalating degeneration of parts of the Reef.

The best place from which to approach the underwater wonderland of the Great Barrier Reef is right where you are now. At its southern end, the Reef is nearly 160 km (100 miles) from the Queensland coast near Rockhampton, and it takes a long boat trip (or a seaplane hop) to reach it. From Cairns, it's but a 20 to 30-km (12 to 20-mile) trip from the Australian mainland to the inner edge of the Reef.

▲▲**Michaelmas Cay**, 45 km (28 miles) northeast of Cairns, is of particular note among the reef islets because it is a tern rook-ery. Thousands of the squawking sea birds circle overhead, pro-tecting their young in their nests, and squabble over shellfish on the isle's sands. (Visitors may carry umbrellas to protect themselves from smelly aerial assaults.) The cay also has superb diving on the offshore Reef.

A Hayles' Cruises launch leaves the Green Island Jetty daily at 8:30 a.m., stops at Green Island for two hours, then continues to Michaelmas Cay. A buffet lunch, snorkeling gear and rides on a submarine-like reef viewer are provided free to all who pay the A$54 fare.

▲▲▲**Hastings Reef** lies on the Reef's outer fringe, where the coral is the youngest and the variety and color of marine life is the greatest. Don't let cloudy weather put you off a trip to this submarine phenomenon, 55 km (34 miles) northeast of Cairns. For one thing, you might not burn as quickly in the less-than-sunny skies. For another, the filtration of rays through the clouds actually brings out the Reef's colors better, especially the blues.

Hayles' Outer Barrier Reef cruise leaves Cairns at 8:30 a.m. daily, stops for two hours at Green Island (where it is joined by Green Island overnighters), does a slow circle around Michael-mas Cay, then anchors at Hastings Reef for three hours. An all-inclusive fare of A$65 includes a buffet lunch, morning and afternoon tea, snorkeling gear (and instruction from a profes-sional dive team), rides on the Reef Pioneer subsea coral viewer and video films of Reef life. Scuba diving equipment can be rented by qualified divers.

DAY 19
CAIRNS TO BRISBANE

The scenic Kuranda Railway will take you inland to the edge of the rainforested Atherton Tableland, climbing steeply above fields of sugar cane to the Barron River Gorge. In Kuranda, you'll have time to see Barron Falls, the open-air market and the Noctarium before returning to Cairns after lunch. Take a late afternoon flight to Brisbane.

Suggested Schedule	
7:30	Breakfast at hotel; store your packed bags.
9:00*	Depart Cairns by rail for Kuranda.
10:30	Arrive Kuranda. Browse through the market, with plenty of time left to see sights of your choice and eat a bite of lunch.
1:30*	Depart Kuranda for Cairns.
3:00	Arrive Cairns. Return to your hotel, pick up your bags and head for the airport.
5:15	Depart Cairns on Ansett Flight #39 to Brisbane. Dinner en route.
7:50	Arrive Brisbane. Check into hotel.
	* Cairns-Kuranda schedule may vary slightly by season.

Sightseeing Highlights
▲▲▲**The Cairns-Kuranda Railway** was an engineering marvel of the late 19th Century. Between 1886 and 1891, a team of more than 1,500 laborers carved this 34-km (21-mile narrow-gauge track from the side of a mountain using pick, shovel and dynamite. They installed 15 tunnels, 98 curves, and dozens of bridges in the 1,055-foot climb from lush canefields up the Barron River Gorge to Kuranda village on the edge of the Atherton Tableland.

Today, tourists can make the same dramatic journey in colonial-style railcars for a round-trip price of A\$10.20. After leaving Cairns (or the alternate restaurant-depot in suburban Freshwater), the train climbs past Horseshoe Bend, with vast views across the checkerboard of canefields to the Coral Sea. (On clear days, you can easily pick out Green Island on the Great Barrier Reef.) After passing Stony Creek Falls, there are breathtaking views of the precipitous Barron River Gorge wherever breaks in the dense rainforest vegetation allow. The train finally emerges at the great Barron Falls, a short distance from Kuranda.

▲**Barron Falls** must have been magnificent before its power-
ful waters were harnessed by a major hydroelectric project. A
small quantity of water is still allowed to trickle over the huge
rock wall—more, of course, during rainy season—to allow
visitors to imagine the former grandeur of this great cataract.
The train makes a photo stop at the Falls Lookout at the end of
the Barron Falls Road from Kuranda. There's also a track from
the lookout to the bottom of the gorge for hiking diehards.
▲**Kuranda Railway Station** is a lovely relic of bygone days.
Built in 1915, it is an oasis in the midst of a tropical jungle, and is
itself a greenhouse of hanging ferns.
▲▲**Kuranda** (pop. 500) lives up to its billing as "the village in
the rainforest." Its tree-lined main street, which leads about a
half-mile from the station to the market, features numerous arts
and crafts galleries and Devonshire tea shops. Horse-drawn
carts ply the short route.

Wednesday and Sundays are market day in Kuranda. The
open-air **Kuranda Market**, winding around a hill and across a
small stream at the west end of town, gives local artisans and
fruit growers a chance to sell their wards and produce. Here's
where you'll find hand-painted T-shirts, leather goods, pottery
and woodwork, as well as tropical delights like mangoes, star-
fruit and custard apples. The market is open rain or shine, April
to October, Wednesdays 9:00 a.m. to noon and Sundays 9:00
a.m. to 1:00 p.m. Nearby is the small **Heritage Homestead**
historical museum (admission A$3).

Across the road from the market is the **Kuranda Wildlife
Noctarium**, an indoor zoo with simulated forest conditions for
nocturnal Australian fauna (admission A$4.50). Also in Kuranda,
you'll find the **Honey House**, where bees in glass hives produce honey sold behind the counter (free admission); the **Cape
York Experience**, an audiovisual program screening daily at
Kurunda Village Centre (admission A$3.50); and the **Jilli Binna
Museum**, a display of artifacts from Aboriginal rainforest
culture (admission 50 cents). The new **Australian Butterfly
Farm**, just out of town, promises to be a major attraction. Back
near the railway station, the *Kurunda Queen* departs hourly for
a 50-minute riverboat cruise on the Barron River (fare A$6.50).

Brisbane Orientation
It has only been in recent years that Brisbane has begun to
outgrow its reputation as a "big country town" and develop a
bit of sophistication. Now that it has tasted the cultured life,
though, it shows no signs of backing off.

Queensland's capital, a city of 1.1 million people, sprawls for
an amazing 471 square miles around both banks of the Brisbane
River. (That makes it the third largest city in the world in area.)

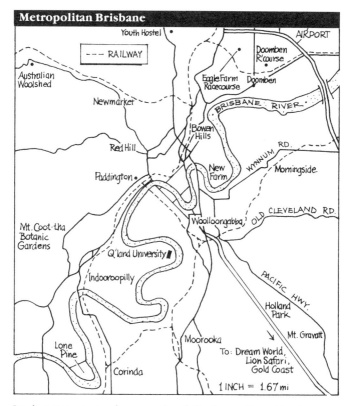

Metropolitan Brisbane

Youth Hostel
AIRPORT
Doomben R'course
--- RAILWAY
Australian Woolshed
Eagle Farm Racecourse
Doomben
BRISBANE RIVER
Newmarket
Bowen Hills
RD.
Red Hill
WYNNUM
New Farm
Morningside
Paddington
OLD CLEVELAND RD.
Woolloongabba
Mt. Coot-tha Botanic Gardens
Q'land University
PACIFIC HWY.
Indooroopilly
Holland Park
Mt. Gravatt
Lone Pine
Moorooka
To: Dream World, Lion Safari, Gold Coast
Corinda
1 INCH = 1.67 mi

Its downtown core, however, is relatively small, swallowing up a single horseshoe bend some 30 km upriver from Moreton Bay.

Like several other Australian cities, Brisbane (pronounced "Briz-b'n") got its start as a convict settlement. British Lieutenant John Oxley founded the colony in 1824. Agricultural and mining wealth from the vast inland reaches of the state made the city prosperous in the late 19th and early 20th centuries. Today, behind (some say in spite of) the leadership of Queensland's controversial, ultra-conservative, 77-year-old premier, John Bjelke-Petersen (you'll hear his name mentioned often), Brisbane has blossomed into a progressive garden city.

The symbol of this newfound refinement is the Queensland Cultural Centre, a brilliant fine and performing arts complex on the banks of the river, across from downtown. It adjoins the riverfront site of World Expo 88, an international exposition in the mold of Vancouver's Expo 86 scheduled to run from April 30 to October 30, 1988.

Brisbane has a subtropical climate, with warm, rainy summers (temperatures range from 67 to 85 degrees Fahrenheit) and drier winters (49 to 69 degrees F).

Most of the main streets in downtown Brisbane have been named after British rulers, so if you know your English history, this should come easy. From the direction of the airport, in northeast Brisbane, Ann Street is the principal thoroughfare leading into downtown. It skirts the central railway station and King George Square, essentially marking the northwestern edge of the city center. Albert Street, running at right angles to Ann Street through the Square, is the main northwest-southeast artery. Ann is paralleled to the southeast by Adelaide, Queen, Elizabeth, Charlotte, Mary, Margaret and Alice streets, with the Botanic Gardens taking the southernmost chunk of the "horseshoe." Albert is paralleled to the southwest by George and William Streets, and to the northeast by Edward, Creek and Wharf Streets. King George Square, on which sits the City Hall, and Queen Street between Albert and Edward are pedestrian malls.

City Transportation

Skennars Transport (tel. 832-1148) provides shuttle-bus service to downtown Brisbane from the domestic and international airport terminals, a distance of some 10 km (6 miles). Buses run half-hourly, and the charge is A$2.70. (You can also catch a No. 160 city bus for 80 cents.) Taxis charge about A$7 over the same distance. Several car-rental agencies have desks at the airport, but you probably won't need one for the remainder of your stay.

Within the city, Queensland Railways' electric Citytrain (tel. 225-0211) and City Council buses (tel. 225-4444) provide service to nearly all points. Six Citytrain lines extend some 45 km (28 miles) east-west from Shorncliffe to Ipswich, 75 km (45 miles) north-south from Caboolture to Beenleigh. Trains operate daily from approximately 4:30 a.m. to 1:30 a.m. (with limited hours on weekends). A one-segment fare is 60 cents. Bus tickets are 50 cents for one zone, 80 cents for two, or you can buy a $3 Day Rover ticket providing unlimited bus transport for one day (5:30 a.m. to 11:30 p.m.). There's also a Brisbane River Ferry Service (tel. 399-4768) providing river crossings at several points for just 40 cents. Brisbane Bicycle Hire, 214 Margaret St. (tel. 229-2592) has bicycles for rent at A$3.50 an hour or A$12 an 8-hour day.

Where to Stay

Brisbane is among the more expensive Australian cities for overnight stays, and it's not getting any cheaper. Its two newest hotels—the **Hilton International**, 190 Elizabeth St. (tel.

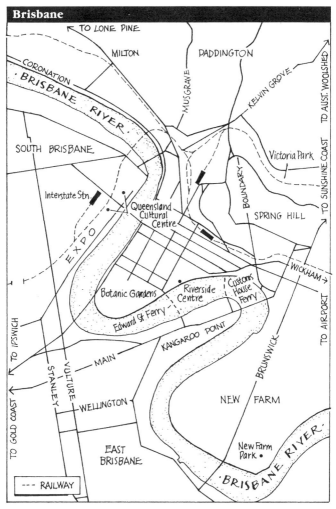

231-3131) and the **Sheraton Brisbane**, 249 Turbot St., (tel. 835-3535)—are luxury world-class accommodations. The Hilton features a 25-story garden atrium, while the 441-room Sheraton looms directly above the central station. A small step down in price is the **Mayfair Crest**, a businessmen's favorite at Ann and Roma streets, King George Square (tel. 229-9111).

The **Brisbane City Travelodge**, Roma Street near George Street (tel. 238-2222), is one of Brisbane's best bargains, with luxury-class facilities at moderate prices. Also centrally located and mid-priced are the **Bellevue Hotel**, 103 George St. (tel. 221-6044); the **Parkview Motel**, 128 Alice St. (tel. 31-2695); and the **Regal Motel**, 132 Alice St. (tel. 31-1541).

The **Yale Budget Inn**, 413 Upper Edward St. (tel. 832-1663), is a bed-and-breakfast guest house extremely popular among economy travelers. **Marrs Town House**, 391 Wickham Terrace (tel. 831-5388), is a newer accommodation near Albert Park while the **Atcherly Hotel**, 513 Queen St. (tel. 832-2591), is an old standby. Budget travelers must book at the downtown YHA office, 462 Queen St., before catching a No. 172 bus north to the **Brisbane Youth Hostel**, 15 Mitchell St. in Kedron (tel. 57-1245), 8 km north of the city center. Much nearer town are the two independent **Brisbane Backpackers Inns** in New Farm, at 71 Kent St. (tel. 385-4504) and 365 Bowen Terrace (tel. 358-1488).

Where to Eat

No one is accusing Brisbane of being the gastronomic capital of Australia. But there are a number of good restaurants, as befits a city of this size.

The southeast Queensland coast is renowned for its seafood—particularly the Moreton Bay bugs (a lobster relation) and the Queensland mud crabs. You can't go wrong ordering them at **Gambaro's**, a causal cafe just west of downtown at 34 Caxton St., Petrie Terrace, or the **Breakfast Creek Wharf**, east of the central city at 160 Breakfast Creek Road, Newstead. Downtown, **Conia's**, 132 Albert St., has excellent seafood.

In the central city area, the best upmarket dining is in the best hotels. **Michael's Riverside**, in the new Riverside Centre at 123 Eagle St., wins plaudits for its highbrow Fench cuisine. But many casual, less expensive spots are fun, too—like **Jimmy's on the Mall**, a licensed open-air restaurant in the Queen Street Mall. In the Elizabeth Arcade off Charlotte Street, **Tortilla** (Aussies pronounce the "L" s) is an atmospheric choice for decent Mexican food and **The Source** has good, cheap vegetarian offerings. **Mama Luigi's**, 240 St. Paul's Terrace, is a longtime Italian favorite, and you can eat like a Russian at **Czars**, 47 Elizabeth St.

The adjacent suburbs of Fortitude Valley and New Farm, walking distance east of downtown (via Ann or Wickham Street), feature many authentic low-priced ethnic restaurants. Try **Giardinetto's** (Italian), 336 Brunswick St.; **Cathay** (Chinese), 222 Wickham St.; **Baan Thai** (Thai), 630 Brunswick St.; and **Possum's** (fair dinkum Aussie), 681 Brunswick St. Further toward the airport, the **Breakfast Creek Hotel**, 2 Kingsford Smith Drive, has a nationally famous steak-and-beer garden.

In Petrie Terrace, **Rag's**, 25 Caxton St., has a reputation as

Brisbane's best French restaurant. The **Caxton Garden Grill**, in the Caxton Hotel, provides jazz accompaniment to meals. In nearby Paddington, the **Elephant Bath**, 183 Given Terrace, offers a rare Asian delight: Sri Lankan curries.

Nightlife

The **Performing Arts Complex**, in the aforementioned Queensland Cultural Centre, comprises the Concert Hall for symphonic performances, the Lyric Theatre for opera, ballet, drama and musical comedy, and the Cremorne Theatre for smaller and experimental productions. Almost any major performance will be presented here. Events scheduled can be obtained, and bookings made, by calling 844-0201 or visiting the PAC box office. The Cultural Centre is on the south side of the Brisbane River at Grey and Melbourne Streets.

Other good spots for live theatre include the **S.G.I.O. Theatre**, Turbot and Albert Streets, home of the Queensland Theatre Company, and **La Boite**, 57 Hale St. in Milton, home of the Brisbane Repertory Company. Queensland film censors are more protective of viewers than other states, but you'll find a good number of movie theatres in the downtown area, especially on Albert Street.

Brisbane's most popular disco-nightclubs, at this writing, were **Sibyl's**, 383 Adelaide St., with three floors of dancing and entertainment; and the **Brisbane Underground**, Caxton and Hal streets in Paddington. Both are open until 3:00 a.m. Wednesdays through Saturdays. The major hotels all have their posh nightspots.

For live music, try the **Hacienda Hotel**, Brunswick and McLachlan Streets in Fortitude Valley, for rock; the **Blue Moon Cafe**, 540 Queen St., for jazz; or the **Treasury Hotel**, Elizabeth and George Streets, for blues. **Wilson's 1870**, 103 Queen St., appeals to an older crowd with a piano bar and cocktail music.

Helpful Hints

The Brisbane Visitors and Convention Bureau (tel. 221-8411), in City Hall on the west side of King George Square, is open weekdays 8:30 a.m. to 5:00 p.m. The Queensland Government Travel Centre is at 196 Adelaide St. (tel. 31-2211), open 9:00 a.m. to 4:45 p.m. Monday to Friday, 9:00 to 11:15 a.m. Saturday. There are tourist information booths in the Queen Street Mall and the Brisbane Transit Centre on Roma Street.

There's an American Consulate at 383 Wickham Terrace (tel. 839-8955). In case of emergencies, dial 000. There's also a 24-hour number for medical service: 378-6900.

DAY 20
BRISBANE AND THE GOLD COAST

Your time is limited, so it's a good day to see the sights from a
city tour bus. Be sure the itinerary includes the Lone Pine Koala
Sanctuary: if you ever wanted a photo of yourself holding one
of these seemingly cuddly creatures, here's where to have it
taken. (In 1988, you may want to spend an extra day in Brisbane
at World Expo '88.) After lunch, take a bus to the Gold Coast,
Australia's answer to Miami Beach. Catch the day's last rays on
the beach.

Suggested Schedule

8:00	Breakfast at hotel.
9:00	Half-day morning tour of city, including the Lone Pine Koala Sanctuary, Mount Coot-tha Gardens and the Queensland Cultural Centre.
12:30	Return from tour. Lunch.
2:00	Board a bus for the Gold Coast.
3:30	Arrive at Surfers Paradise. Check into hotel.
4:30	Hit the beach.
6:30	Relax at hotel.
7:30	Dinner.
9:00	Rage.

Brisbane Sightseeing Highlights

▲▲**City tours** are something I'm not normally crazy about—
mainly because I prefer to explore a new place on my own
time—but given the limited time allotted to Brisbane in this
itinerary, a bus tour is the most efficient way to see the main attractions. Ansett Pioneer Tours (tel. 226-1184) show off the city
sights in a half-day tour leaving major hotels at 9:00 a.m. daily
(fare A$12); Aladdin's Magic Carpet Tours (tel. 345-8300) start
just 15 minutes later (fare A$14). Both "Beautiful Brisbane"
tours last 3 ½ hours. Boomerang Tours' (tel. 221-9922) three-
hour "Morning City Sights" tour (fare A$10) starts at 10:00 a.m.
Saturday, Sunday and Monday only.

▲▲▲**Lone Pine Koala Sanctuary**, on the banks of the
Brisbane River off Jesmond Road in Fig Tree Pocket, 11 km (7
miles) from the city center, has more koalas (over 100) than any
other wildlife reserve in Australia. You can have your photo
taken cuddling one of the creatures (beware the sharp claws),
visit the maternity wing and see newborn koalas, and feed the
freely roaming kangaroos and emus. There are a variety of

other Australian animals, birds and reptiles in the park as well.
Open daily 9:30 a.m. to 5:00 p.m. Adult admission is A$6.50.

You can reach the Lone Pine Sanctuary on your own by taking a No. 84 bus from Adelaide Street. A better way to arrive, if
you've got an afternoon free, is to join the Koala Cruise (tel.
229-7055) leaving daily at 1:15 p.m. from Queens Wharf Road,
North Quay (near downtown). The cruise costs A$9; combined
with a return coach tour, it's A$14.

▲**Mount Coot-tha Botanic Gardens**, Toowong, feature
native and imported plants in the tropical rainforest, subtropical and desert settings. They're open daily 7:00 a.m. to
5:00 p.m. The Sir Thomas Brisbane Planetarium offers a star-
gazing show from Wednesday to Sunday between noon and
7:00 p.m.; bookings are essential. Atop Mount Coot-tha, just 8
km (5 miles) from the city center, is a restaurant with panoramic
views all the way to Moreton Bay. Other major gardens in
Brisbane include the City Botanic Gardens, at the south end of
Albert Street; New Farm Park, east of downtown off Brunswick
Street; and Newstead Park on Breakfast Creek Road, harboring
Brisbane's oldest building, the 1846 Newstead House.

▲▲**The Queensland Cultural Centre** occupies a 14.7-acre
site on the south bank of the Brisbane River, facing the city
center across the Victoria Bridge. A series of distinctive white
structures set amid landscaped gardens, sculptures and water
malls, this A$173 million complex has four components: the
Queensland Art Gallery (opened in 1982), the Performing Arts
Complex (1985), the Queensland Museum (1986), and the State
Library (scheduled for completion in 1988). A convention
center, three restaurants, four cafeterias and several specialty
shops are among its facilities. The Queensland Cultural Centre
Trust (tel. 240-7229) has full information.

The Queensland Art Gallery (tel. 240-7333) displays its permanent collection of Australian and European art, plus numerous touring shows, in 15 separate exhibition areas. A wide
variety of lectures, workshops and musical performances are
regularly offered. There's free admission to the gallery, open
daily 10:00 a.m. to 5:00 p.m., Wednesday to 8:00 p.m. Guided
tours are available weekdays at 11:00 a.m., 1:00 and 2:00 p.m.,
and weekends at 2:00 and 3:00 p.m., for no additional charge.
The 124-year-old **Queensland Museum** (tel. 240-7633) has
three floors of displays emphasizing the state's geology and
natural history, Aboriginal roots and Melanesian influences,
pioneer history and early technology. Popular with children is a
large outdoor Dinosaur Garden. Open daily 9:00 a.m. to 5:00
p.m., Wednesday to 8:00 p.m. Admission is free.

The Performing Arts Complex (tel. 240-7483) attracted
nearly 1 million patrons to its three theatres during its first two

years of operation (see "Nightlife," Day 19). Performers included the Royal Shakespeare Company, the Bolshoi Ballet and the London Philharmonic Orchestra. Guided tours are offered hourly, 10:00 a.m. to 4:00 p.m., Monday to Saturday, for A$2.50. These are backstage tours on selected days by reservation for A$5.

▲**The Australian Woolshed**, 15 km (9½ miles) from downtown at 148 Samford Road, Ferny Hills, is as close as you're likely to get to an authentic Aussie sheep station in a metropolitan area. Working sheepdogs demonstrate their skill, and there are exhibits of wool classing and spinning. There's no admission charge to the complex, open daily 9:30 a.m. to 6:00 p.m., but if you want to see the shearing demonstration and parade of trained rams at 10:45 a.m. daily or 2:00 p.m. Sunday, you'll have to pay A$4.50. The craft shop has been voted Australia's best. A licensed Outback-style restaurant features "bush dances" on Friday and Saturday from 7:00 to midnight.

▲**Earlystreet Historical Village**, 75 McIlwraith Ave., Norman Park, is a collection of eight historic Queensland buildings set in five ares of colonial gardens surrounding the 19th Century Eulalia Manor. You'll find an old slab hut, a shearers' pub, a general store, a blacksmith's shop, a coach house and several residences, all relocated to this site and refurnished in mid-1800s style. Classified by the National Trust, the village is open weekdays 9:30 a.m. to 4:30 p.m., Saturday and Sunday from 10:30 a.m. Admission is A$4.

▲**The Kookaburra Queen** is an elegant wooden paddlewheeler that plies the waters of the Brisbane River several times daily. Ninety-minute tea or snack cruises, leaving at 10:00 a.m. (daily except Saturday), 12:45 p.m. (weekdays) and 3:00 p.m. (Sundays), cost just A$10.90. Daily dinner cruises, boarding at 7:00 p.m., are priced from A$27.90 to A$34.90. The Queen leaves from the Petrie Bight Marina on Howard Street, at the east end of the city near the National Hotel.

The Paddington Circle is the quaintest shopping area in Brisbane. Merchants have retained and restored the suburb's original colonial architecture to give the whole district a heritage feeling. Most of the shops are along Given Terrace and Latrobe Terrace.

World Expo '88

From April 30 to October 30, 1988, Brisbane will host the single largest event in Australian history, the first international exposition to be held in the Southern Hemisphere since the Melbourne World's Fair of 1888. With a theme of "Leisure in the Age of Technology," a projected 30 countries and an equal number of corporations will take part in the fair, expected to attract some 8 million visitors from throughout Australia and overseas.

The 99-acre Expo site spreads for a full kilometer along the south bank of the Brisbane River beside the new Queensland Cultural Centre. Its landmarks are multicolored canopy of polyester "sun sails" raised high above the pavilions and a monorail circling the site. World-class entertainment will perform in a street carnival atmosphere with daily parades and fireworks, circus acts and water shows. A huge amusement park, an artificial lagoon, a manmade mountain of restaurants, and a waterfront stage with riverbank seating for 12,000 people are among the features.

Ticket prices are set at A$25 for one day, A$55 for a three-day pass, A$160 for a season pass, with discounts for early purchase. The Expo grounds will be open from 10:00 a.m. to 10:00 p.m. every day, with extended hours for some restaurants and cabarets. There will be three gates plus a river terminal to serve ferries crossing from downtown. For further information, write World Expo '88, P.O. Box 1988, South Brisbane, Queensland 4101, Australia (tel. 07/840-1988).

Getting To The Gold Coast

Except in the middle of the night, you'll never have to wait longer than an hour or two to catch a bus from Brisbane to Australia's favorite beach resort. Greyhound buses (tel. 240-9333) leave at least 10 times a day from the Roma Street Transit Centre. Skennars Transport (tel. 832-1148) also has several buses departing daily for the Gold Coast from its depot on Barry Parade near Fortitude Valley. The fare is A$8.10, whether you head for Southport (1 hour 15 minutes), Surfers Paradise (1½ hours) or Coolangatta (about two hours).

There's talk of opening a rail link between Brisbane and the Gold Coast, but at this writing it's still at least a year from completion.

Gold Coast Orientation

A glittering white-sand beach stretching 32 km (20 miles) down the coast of southeasternmost Queensland, just 65 km (40 miles) from Brisbane, the Gold Coast is the single most popular resort strip in Australia. That has both good and bad connotations. There are hotels, restaurants and nightspots of all standards and prices, a lush mountain backdrop not far from the lovely beach, and an incredible variety of man-made attractions. But there's also a great deal of crass commercialism and tourist kitsch preying on the throngs in transition. Overlook that and you'll have a great time.

At least a dozen separate communities, linked by the busy Gold Coast Highway, comprise the City of Gold Coast. About

200,000 people make their home along this narrow strip, four times the population of 20 years ago. Southport, the Gold Coast's northernmost community, is its commercial and industrial center. Surfers Paradise, the next main center reached heading south, is the Waikiki-style high-rise capital of the coast, and the site of its most frenetic nightlife. Halfway down the coast is Burleigh Heads, a laid-back family community at the foot of fauna-rich Burleigh Heads National Park. Coolangatta marks not only the southern extreme of the Gold Coast, but also the boundary between Queensland and New South Wales. The Gold Coast Airport, with direct links to Sydney, Melbourne, Adelaide and other cities, is here.

Local Transportation
Don't worry about being stuck on the Gold Coast without a car. You can either base yourself in one town and cope quite nicely, or you can call upon Surfside buses (tel. 36-2449) for regular transportation links between Southport and Coolangatta. No fare is higher than A$2. Smekels Busline (tel. 32-6211) serves the Southport area more thoroughly, but doesn't go further south than Broadbeach. Silly Style, 6 Beach Road, Surfers, will rent you a bike or moped.

Where To Stay
As Surfers Paradise (usually called "Surfers") is the center of most of the action, we'll deal with it first. At the top of the line are the elegant **Ramada At Paradise Center**, Gold Coast Highway and Hanlan Street (tel. 075/59-34000) and the **Holiday Inn-Surfers Paradise**, 22 View St. (tel. 59-1000). The **Chevron Paradise Hotel**, Ferny Avenue (tel. 39-0444), is a good choice in the moderate price bracket. You're reaching a bit to find a decent economy room in Surfers, but the **Hub Motel**, 21 Cavill Ave. (tel. 31-5559) will do quite nicely. The nearest budget accommodation to Surfers is the AYH hostel in the **El Dorado Motel**, 2821 Gold Coast Highway (tel. 31-5155), nearly a mile south of Surfers. You must check in between 4:00 and 6:00 p.m.

Outside of Surfers, the best accommodation is the **Conrad International Hotel**, Gold Coast Highway, Broadbeach Island (tel. 92-1133). It's the site of Jupiter's Casino. You'll find moderate and economy-priced motels all along the Gold Coast Highway from here south, but Coolangatta is the king in these price ranges. Try the **Pacific Village Hotel**, 88 Marine Parade (tel. 36-2733), or the **Bombora Holiday Lodge**, Marine Parade at Dutton Street (tel. 36-1888). The **Backpackers Inn**, 45 McLean St., Coolangatta (tel. 36-2422), costs less than A$8 a night and has a licensed restaurant and bar on the premises.

Where to Eat
There are as many different kinds of places to eat on the Gold
Coast as there are kinds of people who visit, and that's a lot.
The coast's characterization as a utopia for junk-food junkies is
not totally inaccurate, but there is no shortage of more whole-
some dining establishments.

In Surfers, try the **Rusty Pelican**, Orchid and Elkhorn
avenues, or the **Captain's Tale**, 5 Cavill Ave. on the mall, for
seafood; **Pellegrini**, 3120 Gold Coast Highway, for Italian
cuisine; or **Shogun**, 90 Bundall Road, for Japanese food. Be
warned, however: none of them are cheap. You can spend less
money and have a lot of fun at the hofbrau-style **Bavarian
Steak House**, Gold Coast Highway at Cavill Avenue; the **Tan-
doori Taj** (North Indian), 3100 Gold Coast Highway; the **Mexican Kitchen**, 150 Bundall Road; or the **Athens** (Greek), Gold
Coast Highway near Laycock Street. The **Surfer's Deli**, 25 Orchid Avenue, is a pleasant sidewalk cafe with light meals and
entertainment.

Up and down the coast the **Holy Mackerel**, 174 Marine
Parade, Labrador (north of Southport), offers free shuttle service from Surfers to its seafood restaurant. Mermaid Beach has a
good Italian restaurant, **Gino's Osteria**, 2563 Gold Coast
Highway, and nearby on the same road, the most passionately
named vegetarian eatery I've ever heard of—the **Lusty Lentil**.
Further down, in Burleigh Heads, the **Chieng Mai Thai**
restaurant is at 31 James St. Finally, no south end budget watcher
should pass up a $3.30 counter meal at the **Queensland Hotel**,
Boundary Street, Coolangatta.

Nightlife
The cards are dealt 24 hours a day at **Jupiter's Casino** in the
Conrad International Hotel on Broadbeach Island. Blackjack,
roulette, craps, baccarat, keno, and several other games are
played continuously in this sophisticated new casino. There are
also several restaurants and a showroom featuring world-class
entertainers.

In Surfers, the overloaded disco-cabaret lineup includes such
standouts as **Twains International** and the five-story **Pent-
house**, both on Orchid venue. The **Swingin' Vine**, 47A Cavill
Ave., is noted for jazz and comedy. Ask for directions to **Bom-
bay Rock**, the best of several clubs in Surfers that feature live
rock. It's counterpart, 13 km (8 miles) south of Surfers in North
Palm Beach, is the **Playroom**, on the Gold Coast Highway opposite the Tallebudgera Bridge.

There's cheaper entertainment just across the New South
Wales border from Coolangatta, in the town of Tweed Heads.
The club scene flourishes here where poker machines ("one-

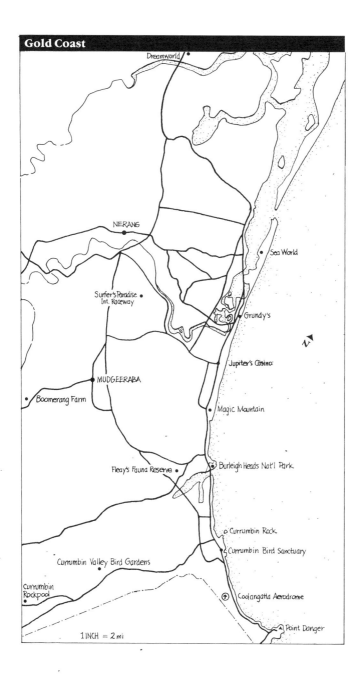

Gold Coast

Dreamworld

NERANG

Sea World

Surfer's Paradise
Int. Raceway

Grundy's

N

Jupiter's Casino

MUDGEERABA

Boomerang Farm

Magic Mountain

Burleigh Heads Nat'l Park

Fleay's Fauna Reserve

Currumbin Rock

Currumbin Bird Sanctuary

Currumbin Valley Bird Gardens

Currumbin
Rockpool

Coolangatta Aerodrome

Point Danger

1 INCH = 2 mi

armed bandits'') are legal. Meals, drinks and top-flight entertainment are always reduced in price to entice you to play the polies. They're technically membership clubs, but out-of-state visitors, especially foreigners, are welcomed. Shuttle buses can run you from Surfers or elsewhere on the Gold Coast to such spots as **Twin Towns Services Club**, Wharf Street; **Tweed Heads Bowls Club**, Tweed Street; and my favorite, **Seagulls Rugby League Football Club**, Gollan Drive.

For romancers or real budget watchers, there's nothing cheaper than a walk on a moonlit beach.

Helpful Hints
The Gold Coast Visitors and Convention Bureau has its main offices in the Cavill Mall, Surfers Paradise (tel. 38-4419). (There's a Coolangatta branch: tel. 26-7765). You'll also find the Queensland Government Travel Centre here on the second floor of the TAA Building, 38-40 Cavill Ave. (tel. 92-1033). All are open 9:00 a.m. to 4:45 p.m. weekdays, 9:00 to 11:15 a.m. Saturday.

The Surfers Paradise post office is at the corner of Cavill Avenue and the Gold Coast Highway. Banking hours are 9:30 a.m. to 4:00 p.m. Monday to Thursday, to 5:00 p.m. Friday. Retail shops are open daily except Sunday, 9:00 a.m. to 5:30 p.m.

In case of emergencies, dial 000. For 24-hour medical assistance, call 38-8823.

DAY 21
THE GOLD COAST

Your final day on Asutralian beaches. Why not decide for
yourself if the name "Surfers Paradise" really fits? Or dive into a
grab bag of tourist attractions like Sea World, the Currumbin
Bird Sanctuary or the Mudgeeraba Boomerang Farm.

Suggested Schedule	
7:30	Up and at 'em, unless you need extra sleep to recover from last night's fling.
9:00	Visit the Currumbin Sanctuary near Palm Beach.
11:00	Catch a few late morning rays.
12:30	Lunch
1:30	Sea World is worth a full afternoon.
5:00	Head back to your hotel. Take a quick dip in the pool.
6:30	Dinner.
8:00	It's your last night in Australia—what you do with it is up to you.

Sightseeing Highlights
▲▲**The Currumbin Sanctuary**, just off the Gold Coast Highway on Tomewin Street, Currumbin, 18 km (11 miles) south of
Surfers, is a tourist favorite mainly because of the flocks of
brightly colored rainbow Lorikeets which fly in daily from their
homes in the wild to be fed from plates of honey by willing
visitors. Arrive before 10:00 a.m. to see the mass of orange-
breasted, blue-headed, green-backed birds, or wait until about
4:00 in the afternoon. A variety of other native birds, koalas,
kangaroos and wallabies make their homes in the 50-acre
wildlife refuge. You can walk among the critters or watch from a
2-km miniature railway. Numerous craftsmen ply their trades;
among them are potters, glass blowers and gem cutters. Open
daily 8:00 a.m. to 5:00 p.m. Adult admission is A$8.
▲▲**Sea World**, on the Spit 5 km (3 miles) north of Surfers, is
Australia's No. 1 marine theme park. Dolphins, killer whales and
sea lions alternately awe and amuse audiences in separate
shows, as do acrobatic water skiers. The World of the Sea
Theatre combines audiovisuals with live demonstrations of
underwater diving and shark feeding. Visitors can pet dolphins,
feed sea lions and gaze at an enormous aquarium. The park's
dozen rides include Australia's first free-fall waterslide (with a
frightening five-story drop!) and its only triple-loop roller-

coaster, as well as a monorail and carousel for those of less intestinal fortitude.

Sea World is open daily (except Christmas) from 10:00 a.m. to 5:00 p.m. The adult admission of A$18 includes all rides and performances. Call 32-1055 or 32-5131 (recorded) for daily showtimes and bus connections.

Dreamworld, in Coomera 15 minutes toward Brisbane from Surfers, is Australia's largest Disney-style theme park. This 208-acre complex has a little of everything, some of which will remind you very much of parks in Anaheim and Orlando. You can see the Koala Country Music Show, for example, with 22 life-size but computerized Aussie animals doing the singing and playing. You can take any of 17 different rides, among them a steam train, a "Murrissippi River" cruise and a high-speed trip through Avalanche Mountain. Sound familiar? Seventeen shops and 11 restaurants take care of shopping and hunger pangs.

Dreamworld is open Saturday to Wednesday, 10:00 a.m. to 5:00 p.m., daily during school holiday periods. Adult admission of A$15 includes all rides and performances. Round-trip express bus service from the Gold Coast is offered for A$6 by Keith's Tours (tel. 30-5908).

Magic Mountain, on the Gold Coast Highway at Nobby's Beach near Miami, is another man-made attraction of the same ilk. You can't miss seeing the medieval castle atop the bluff long before you arrive. The numerous rides include a chairlift to carry you to the mountaintop for panoramic views of the Gold Coast. But the highlight of a visit is "Visions," a superb show presented by magician and illusionist Arthur Coghlan. Open Sunday to Thursday, 10:00 a.m. to 5:00 p.m., daily in summer and during school holiday periods. Adult admission of A$10.50 includes all rides and shows. Call 52-2333 to arrange free bus pickup from hotels.

Burleigh Heads National Park is a small, unexpected natural bushland oasis in the middle of this utterly commercial strip. Koalas, wallabies, bandicoots and much birdlife inhabit this bluff overlooking the mouth of Tallebuddgera Creek. A graded 3-km (2-mile) walking track leads around the headland.

Mudgeeraba Boomerang Farm, on Springbrook Road 20 minutes inland from the Gold Coast, is not a major tourist attraction. Unlike others, however, it's uniquely Australian. Not only will the Hawes family sell you a boomerang made in their own factory; they'll teach you how to throw it so that it comes back to you. Their 200-acre farm also has a fascinating boomerang museum. Open seven days week. Ask directions locally or phone 30-5231.

▲**Lamington National Park** comprises some 50,000 acres of lushly forested mountains 43 km (27 miles) from the Gold Coast via Nerang. Some call it "the Green behind the Gold." The park contains 140 km (87 miles) of walking tracks, an estimated 500 waterfalls, and a forest of 3,000-year-old beech trees. Two small guest houses, at Binna Burra and O'Reilly's, serve park visitors.

Grundy's at Paradise Centre is the sort of place that shoppers and fun-seekers don't need to be told about: they'll find it on their own. Set dead center in Surfers Paradise, with direct access from the beach, Ramada Hotel or Cavill Mall, this three-story complex includes 110 boutiques and specialty shops, an international food village, and the most cacophonous collection of video games you've ever heard (or seen).

Pacific Fair, near the casino-hotel in Broadbeach, is the Gold Coast's other most interesting shopping center. The architects have recreated streets from all over the world—from Oxford Street (London) to the Boulevarde St. Michel (Paris), Basin Street (New Orleans) to Lindenstrasse (Berlin). Appropriate specialty shops intermingled with chain department stores.

DAY 22
FLY HOME FROM BRISBANE

It's been a great 22 days. Board your flight home to the States in Brisbane this afternoon. Thanks to the International Date Line, you'll reach the U.S. West Coast only 1½ hours after leaving Australia. The longest day of your life was custom-made for savoring those great Australian memories.

Suggested Schedule

8:00	Rise and shine, eat breakfast, and pack everything but your bathing suit.
9:00	You've got three hours left for the beach.
12:00	Grab a Vegemite sandwich for lunch, scoop up your bags and board a bus for Brisbane airport.
1:30	Arrive at the airport for check-in.
3:00	Qantas Flight No. 25 leaves for Honolulu, with connections there to San Francisco, Los Angeles and other cities in the U.S. and Canada.

Farewell Advice

Call your airline first thing in the morning to reconfirm your departure time. Hopefully, you will also have telephoned a couple days earlier from Brisbane to confirm your seat.

The buses of Skennars Transport (tel. 38-9444 in Surfers, 36-2574 in Coolangatta) offer direct shuttle service from the Gold Coast to Brisbane International Airport. The fare is A$8.10. Remember to allow 1½ hours for the trip from Surfers, two hours from Coolangatta.

When you reach Brisbane, instruct the driver that you need the international terminal. The domestic terminal, where you arrived, is a considerable drive away, around the runways.

Don't spend all your money before reaching the airport. You'll have to hold A$20 out to pay the airport departure tax.

As you head back home across the Pacific, you can think back on a great three-week vacation—and where you want to go on your next trip Down Under.

POST TOUR OPTIONS

The biggest frustration in trying to cover an entire continent in 22 days is omitting so many worthwhile spots from the itinerary. If you've got the time, the following five options can be spliced into your schedule as follows:

Tasmania—Leave from and return to Melbourne (Day 8).

Adelaide and/or **Perth**—Between Melbourne and Alice Springs (Day 11).

Darwin—Between Alice Springs and Cairns (Day 16).

Barrier Reef Islands—Between Cairns and Brisbane (Day 19).

TASMANIA

Australia's island state, some 230 km (143 miles) across Bass Strait from Victoria, is almost a world unto itself. Like a cross between New England and the Pacific Northwest, its colonial manors are scattered through the lowlands beneath forested mountain peaks.

Suggested 6-Day Schedule	
DAY 1	Arrive in Devonport from Melbourne. Rent a car and drive to Launceston.
DAY 2	See Cataract Gorge, then drive down the east coast via Campbelltown to Point Arthur.
DAY 3	After exploring the former penal colony in the morning, drive to Hobart via Richmond.
DAY 4	Catch the view from Mount Wellington, then drive via Lake St. Clair and Queenstown to Strahan.
DAY 5	Go on the Gordon River cruise in the morning, then drive to Stanley for the night.
DAY 6	Putter down the north coast to Devonport. Night flight or ferry voyage back to Melbourne.

Getting There

Two to five flights daily transit the Bass Strait between Melbourne and Hobart (the state capital), Launceston, Devonport, and Burnie/Wynyard. The flight takes 65 minutes to Hobart, 55 minutes to Launceston, 50 minutes to the other two north coast towns. The lowest round-trip fares, at this writing, were A\$192 to Hobart, A\$165 to Launceston, A\$146 to Devonport and Burnie/Wynyard, on a 30-day advance purchase excursion basis. (If you're under 25, **East-West Airlines** will give you a 20% dis-

count.) There are also direct flights several times a week to
Launceston and Hobart from Sydney and the Gold Coast.

An overnight ferry, the *Abel Tasman*, crosses the strait three
times a week, leaving Melbourne at 6 p.m. Monday, Wednesday
and Friday and arriving in Devonport at 8:30 the following
morning. Return boats leave Devonport at 6 p.m. Tuesday,
Thursday and Sunday. One-way fares vary according to season
and facilities, but range from A$75 (winter) to A$109 (summer)
on the low end to A$141 to A$197 at the high end.

Getting Around
The large auto rental firms—Hertz, Avis and Budget—are represented in all large towns in Tasmania. Weekly rates, including
unlimited kilometers, are similar, ranging from A$282 to A$600
depending upon class of vehicle. You'll get a better deal from
Advance Travel Car Rentals in Devonport (tel. 004/24-8885)

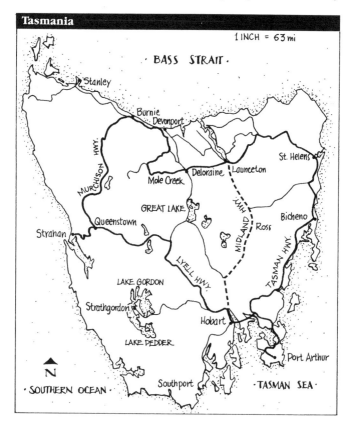

or Launceston (tel. 003-44-2164), with weekly rates starting at A$144.

If you're a solo budget traveler, look into the seven-day "Tassie Pass" with **Tasmanian Redline Coaches** for A$60. (A 14-day pass is only A$75.) Book through Tasbureau (see "Helpful Hints"). The Redline terminal to Devonport is at 9 Edward St. (tel. 004/24-2585); in Launceston at 112 George St. (tel. 003/31-9177); in Hobart at 96 Harrington St. (tel. 004/34-4577).

Sightseeing Highlights
▲**Devonport**—(Pop. 25,000) is the market center of the fertile north coast region. **Tiagarra**, atop the headland called Mersey Bluff, remembers the culture of the Tasmanian Aboriginal, one of the most tragic races in history. Early settlers hunted down and shot the native Tasmanians until a mere handful survived. They were resettled off Tasmania's north coast, on Flinders Island, where the last one died in 1876. Also in Devonport are the **Don River Railway Museum**, the **Maritime Museum**, and **Taswegia** historic printery and craft gallery.
▲**Launceston**—Is Tasmania's second city, both in population (65,000) and age (founded in 1805, a year after Hobart). Situated at the head of the tranquil Tamar River, it is noted for its many parks and gardens, especially **Cataract Gorge**. Reminiscent of the Wisconsin Dells, it is surrounded by a rhododendron garden and crossed by an aerial chairlift. Also see the **Queen Victoria Museum and Art Gallery** and the **Waverly Woollen Mills** (tours daily 9 a.m. to 4 p.m.) Thirteen km (8 miles) west of Launceston, near Hadspen, is the beautiful **Entally House** historic homestead, built in 1819.
▲▲▲**Port Arthur**—Was a name synonymous with harsh justice in Australia's convict past. Between 1830 and 1877, some 12,500 hardened criminals lived in this isolated location under the threat of the lash and long-term solitary isolation that drove many to madness. Today, the restored **Port Arthur National Historic Site** commemorates the nation's roots like nowhere else.

Elsewhere on the Tasman Peninsula, you can see spectacular coastal formations—arches, undersea caves and blowholes—that helped make this prison colony so difficult to escape. **The Bush Mill** theme park, 5 km (3 miles) north of the historic site, recalls the days of the early timber cutters. The **Tasmanian Devil Park** at Taranna, another 5 km north, is a good place to see these varmints.
▲▲**Richmond**—Is a detour off the road back to Hobart, just 26 km (16 miles) northeast of the capital. The treasures of this charming 1820s town include Australia's first bridge and its

oldest Catholic church. The Richmond Gaol has been faithfully restored. Many of the community's elegant sandstone buildings now house Devonshire tea shops, arts and crafts galleries and historical museums.

▲▲▲**Hobart**—Tasmania's capital and largest city (pop. 175,000) was established in 1804 as the second European settlement in Australia. The inner-city suburb of **Battery Point** is the original seamen's quarter, where tiny cottages share the narrow winding streets with Georgian mansions and Victorian terrace houses—now, as often as not, occupied by restaurants, bed-and-breakfasts, art galleries and antique shops. **The Van Diemen's Land Memorial Folk Museum** in the Narryna mansion at 103 Hampden Road has a superb period collection. The **Maritime Museum of Tasmania** in the Secheron House mansion off Colville Street is also interesting.

Elsewhere in Hobart, see the excellent **Tasmanian Museum and Art Gallery**, the **Royal Tasmanian Botanical Gardens** and the scale-model **Tudor Court** at Sandy Bay. From the summit of 4,170-foot **Mount Wellington**, a 20-km (12 ½ -mile) drive from the city center, you can savor the spectacular layout of this beautiful harbor city at the mouth of the Derwent River.

▲▲**Strahan**—A tiny fishing and timber port, is best known as the starting point for cruises through Macquarie Habour and up the Gordon River, a crystalline stream that winds through unexplored rainforest from **South West National Park**. Mount Everest conqueror Sir Edmund Hillary has called this region "the greatest walking country in the world." Some believe its denizens may include the legendary Tasmanian wolf, a striped marsupial canine last confirmed alive in the 1930s.

▲**Stanley**—Has changed little since it was established in 1826 by sheep breeders. Its combination of history and maritime beauty is accented by **The Nut**, a striking 500-foot mesa-like basalt outcropping that dominates coastal scenery for many miles around.

▲**The Northwest Coast** drive—129 km (80 miles) along the Bass Highway from Stanley to Devonport, provides a final day of Tasmanian wanderings. **Rocky Cape National Park** contains Aboriginal caves, fields of wild orchids, and the glistening white-sand **Sisters Beach** with Birdland Native Gardens reserve. **Lapoinya** rhododendron gardens are nearby. At **Wynyard**, you'll find **Fossil Bluff**, where the oldest marsupial fossil in Australia was discovered. **Burnie** (pop. 21,000) has a major timber products industry and the **Pioneer Village Museum**, recreating the town's turn-of-the-century commercial center. Proceed east to the town of **Penguin**, which takes its name from colonies of fairy penguins living along the shore; **Ulverstone**, gateway to the Leven Canyon; and finally to **Devonport** and the Abel Tasman ferry terminal.

Helpful Hints

Tasmania calls its state tourist agency **Tasbureau**. The head office is at 80 Elizabeth St., Hobart (tel. 002-30-0211), but you'll find other offices along the route in Devonport (18 Rooke St., tel. 004/24-1526); Launceston (St. John and Paterson streets, tel. 003/32-2101); Queenstown (39 Orr St., tel. 004/71-1009); and Burnie (48 Cattley St., tel. 004/30-2224). Most of these offices are open from 8:45 a.m. to 5:45 p.m. weekdays, 9 to 11 a.m. Saturdays.

In Melbourne, Tasbureau is at 256 Collins St. (tel. 03/63-6351) and in Sydney, at 129 King St. (tel. 02/233-2500). In North America, write c/o the Australian Tourist Commission, Suite 1740, 3550 Wilshire Blvd., Los Angeles, CA 90010 (tel. 213/380-6060).

Two publications produced by Tasbureau are invaluable. "The Visitor's Guide to Tasmania" will tell you about every tourist attraction in the state. The bimonthly "Tasmanian Travelways" newspaper tells you how to get there, where to stay and where to eat, and how much it will cost you.

ADELAIDE AND SOUTH AUSTRALIA

South Australia calls itself the "WOW" state—wine, opals and wildlife. The Barossa Valley northeast of Adelaide is Australia's premier wine-producing district; Coober Pedy, in the state's scorching outback, is the country's best-known opal-mining center; and Kangaroo Island, off the south coast, may have a richer concentration of native fauna than any other part of the nation.

Adelaide, the pleasant capital of South Australia, is a perfect staging point for reaching these and other outlying attractions. Though Adelaide, with few points of major tourist interest, may come across to visitors as "a big country town," its urban population of 900,000 is two-thirds that of the entire state. The city center is lovely, carefully platted beside the River Torrens and completely surrounded by a ring of spacious parkland.

I won't suggest a schedule here, since South Australia's attractions are in various directions from Adelaide and may not be practical to include in one itinerary without considerable time and/or money. Pick and choose spots that pique your interest.

Getting There

The major domestic carriers, Ansett and Australian Airlines, serve Adelaide with nonstop daily flights to and from Sydney, Melbourne, Perth and Alice Springs, and regularly scheduled direct flights to and from Brisbane, Canberra, Darwin, the

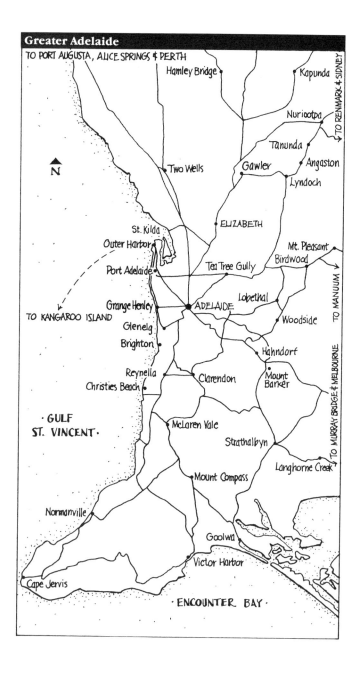

Greater Adelaide

TO PORT AUGUSTA, ALICE SPRINGS & PERTH

Hamley Bridge

Kapunda

TO RENMARK & SIDNEY

Nuriootpa

Tanunda

Two Wells

Gawler

Angaston

Lyndoch

N

ELIZABETH

St. Kilda

Mt. Pleasant

Outer Harbor

Birdwood

Port Adelaide

Tea Tree Gully

TO MANNUM

Grange Henley

ADELAIDE

Lobethal

TO KANGAROO ISLAND

Glenelg

Woodside

Brighton

Hahndorf

Reynella

Clarendon

Mount Barker

Christies Beach

GULF ST. VINCENT

McLaren Vale

Strathalbyn

TO MURRAY BRIDGE & MELBOURNE

Langhorne Creek

Mount Compass

Normanville

Goolwa

Cape Jervis

Victor Harbor

ENCOUNTER BAY

Gold Coast and Queensland's Sunshine Coast. Air time from Sydney is about 1 hour, 50 minutes; from Perth, it's about 3 hours. South Australian time is 30 minutes ahead of Sydney, Melbourne and Brisbane, but 1½ hours behind Western Australia. Several small carriers ply local routes; most notable is Kendall Airlines, which flies an Adelaide-Coober Pedy-Ayers Rock service every Saturday morning.

You can rent a vehicle and drive directly from Melbourne, 747 km (464 miles) via the Western and Dukes highways, or Sydney, 1,433 km (890 miles) via the Mid Western and Stuart highways). Brisbane is 2,056 km (1,277 miles) by the shortest route, Alice Springs is 1,697 km (1,054 miles), and if you're really adventurous, Perth is 2,720 km (1,690 miles) across the treacherous Nullarbor Plain. (Null arbor = "no vegetation.") Interstate buses ply these highways daily.

Rail service is also regular and efficient, with daily connections from Melbourne and Perth, six days a week from Sydney, and the famous "Ghan" weekly from Alice Springs.

Getting Around

You can rent a car at the airport or take the half-hourly Transit Regency coach into the city for A$2.40. Once you've arrived in Adelaide, the public transportation system—called the *State Transport Authority* (12A Grenfell St., tel. 210-1000)—will take good care of you. Buses run north to Elizabeth, south to Reynella, and east through the many communities of the Adelaide Hills. Suburban trains operate over a wider area, while the city's only electric tram links downtown with the seaside suburb of Glenelg. The interconnecting services run from 6 a.m. to 11:30 p.m. Monday to Saturday, 9 a.m. to 10:30 p.m. Sunday. Fares start at 70 cents. The *Adelaide Explorer Bus* (tel. 212-7344) stops at eight points on a 34-km (21-mile) circuit around the city; passengers who pay the A$6 adult fare can freely board and disembark over the course of the day.

Adelaide Highlights

It makes sense for Adelaide visitors to focus their sightseeing attentions on **North Terrace**, the broad thoroughfare which demarcates the north end of downtown. On or near this street, you'll find the Adelaide Casino, Constitutional Museum, The Festival Centre, Government House, State Library, South Australian Museum, Art Gallery of South Australia, University of Adelaide, Ayers House and the Botanic Gardens—all within a five-block stretch.

▲The **South Australian Maritime Museum**, 119 Lipson St., Port Adelaide, has an enormous collection of marine artifacts documenting South Australia's maritime history.

▲**Glenelg** is Adelaide's most famous beach, a short trip from the city center by tram. Capt. John Windmarsh landed here and proclaimed the colony of South Australia in 1836; a replica of his boat, the *HMS Buffalo*, contains restaurants and a museum. Down the shore is a major amusement center, Magic Mountain.

▲**Carrick Hill**, 590 Fullarton Road, Springfield, a circa-1939 Elizabethan-style manor house surrounded by 96 acres of gardens and bushland, contains a priceless private art collection of 19th and 20th Century oils, silver, pewter and furniture.

▲▲▲The **Adelaide Hills** rise above the coastal plain 20 minutes' drive east of the city center. Their charm is in their views, bushland reserves and numerous unique villages scattered through the gentle valleys. **Hahndorf**, 28 km (17 miles) from Adelaide, was founded in 1839 by German refugees and is still "sehr Deutsch": many original stone buildings house hotels, restaurants and artisans' studios. **Birdwood Mill National Motor Museum** at Birdwood has 300 vintage vehicles and other antiques in an old flour mill. **Cleland Conservation Park**, on the slopes of 2,333-foot Mount Lofty, is a great place for bushwalking and for viewing native wildlife.

South Australia Highlights

▲▲▲The **Barossa Valley**—Is the largest wine-producing district in Australia's major wine-producing state. Fifty separate wineries, most of them located in a stretch of 23 km (14 miles) along the Barossa Valley Highway between Lyndoch and Nuriootpa, open their cellar doors daily for tastings of their exquisite clarets and rieslings. The center of the region is Tanunda, a German town established in 1843 and the focus of the Barossa Valley Vintage Festival, held in April of every odd-numbered year (i.e. 1989, 1991).

▲▲The **Flinders Ranges**—Comprise a majestic set of sharp granite peaks and deep gorges 350 to 620 km (215 to 385 miles) north of Adelaide. Within this wilderness are ancient Aboriginal sites, abandoned mining towns, geological oddities, two national parks (Flinders Ranges and Gammon) and the Wilpena Pound, an enormous natural amphitheater surrounded by steep cliffs.

▲▲▲**Coober Pedy**—Is one of the world's most unusual communities. Most of the 2,100 residents of this opal-mining town, 943 km (586 miles) northwest of Adelaide by road, live in underground "dugouts" (homes) to escape the blistering desert heat. (The town's name derives from an Aboriginal phrase, "kupa piti," meaning "white man's hole.") More than half the world's opals are mined at Coober Pedy. You can see demonstrations of opal cutting and polishing, or even get a budget bed, at the Umoona Mine; explore an underground display home and church, visit a museum, and shop for raw or cut opals. Coober Pedy is a good overnight stop between Adelaide and Alice Springs.

▲▲**Kangaroo Island**—Australia's third-largest offshore island, is best known for its plentiful wildlife. Some 150 km (90 miles) long, it is connected to Adelaide by four flights a day (A$84 return) and a daily ferry from Port Adelaide (A$29, leaving at 10 a.m., arriving at 11:30 a.m.). The main town, Kingscote, is a farming center, but the main visitor draw is Flinders Chase National Park, where kangaroos, koalas, emus and other native species run wild. Divers enjoy exploring offshore shipwrecks; fishing, bushwalking and sunning on the beaches are also popular.

▲▲The **Murray River** is Australia's "Old Man River." Longer, at 1,609 miles, than any U.S. river except the Mississipi, Yukon and Missouri, it drains almost 1/7 of the Australian continent. Its final (and broadest) 400 miles cut through South Australia, emptying into Lake Alexandrina and Encounter Bay just south of Tailem Bend. You can cruise the river aboard a fully-contained paddle wheeler like the *Proud Mary*, which sails between Murray Bridge and Renmark on 5-day or overnight cruises (33 Pirie St., Adelaide; tel. 08/51-9472); or rent your own houseboat: contact the Lower Murray Regional Tourist Association, P.O. Box 344, Murray Bridge, SA 5253 (tel. 085/32-6660), for booking details.

Helpful Hints

The **South Australian Government Travel Centre**, 18 King William St. near North Terrace (tel. 212-1644), operates a free information and booking service for hotels and tours throughout Adelaide and the state. It's open Monday to Friday 8:15 a.m. to 5:30 p.m., weekends and holidays 9 a.m. to 2 p.m.

PERTH AND WESTERN AUSTRALIA

Perth doesn't fit neatly into a 22-day itinerary merely because of its isolation from the rest of Australia. Adelaide, some 2,200 km (1,400 miles) distant (by air), is the nearest city with more than 25,000 people, and Jakarta, Indonesia, is closer to Perth than the Australian national capital, Canberra.

For those with time, however, it's well worth a visit. Perth, where 1 million of the 1.4 million Western Australians live, is a lovely Mediterranean-style city nestled along the shores of the broad Swan River. Best known in recent years as the temporary (1983-1987) home of the America's Cup of yachting, Perth is the gateway to a vast and varied state larger in itself than France.

Suggested Schedule	
DAY 1	Arrive in Perth. Enjoy a walking tour of the city, from London Court to Kings Park.
DAY 2	Spend the day in Fremantle, an atmospheric European-style port town and the site of the 1987 America's Cup yacht races.
DAY 3	Cruise the Swan River, passing the Royal Perth Yacht Club and continuing to Rottnest Island, where you can bicycle among the quokkas.
DAY 4	Final sightseeing before an onward flight.

Getting There

Ansett and Australian Airlines have nonstop daily flights to Perth from Adelaide, Melbourne and Sydney, and regular direct flights from Brisbane, Cairns, Mount Isa, Alice Springs, Darwin and Port Hedland. Air time from Sydney is about 4½ hours, from Adelaide around 3 hours. (Perth time is 2 hours behind Sydney and Melbourne, 1½ behind Adelaide and the Northern Territory.) Think twice before driving across the seemingly endless Western Australian desert to Perth. Taking the train, however, is a wise alternative to flying. The "Indian-Pacific" takes 66 hours from Sydney, via Broken Hill, Adelaide and Kalgoorlie, three times a week; the "Trans-Australian" runs 38 hours from Adelaide (with connections from Melbourne) twice a week.

Getting Around

Rent a car at the airport, 11 km (7 miles) from downtown, take the Skybus coach to downtown Perth or major hotels for A$3.50, or catch a city bus. The public transportation system, called **Transperth** (125 St. George's Terrace, tel. 221-1211) operates buses and trains weekly from 6 a.m. to 7:15 p.m., with reduced wervices on weekends and holidays. Tickets good for two hours on all services cost A$1. Free buses circle the city at 10-minute intervals from 7 a.m. to 5:30 p.m. weekdays, 9 to 11:30 a.m. Saturdays.

Perth Sightseeing Highlights

▲▲A walk down **St. George's Terrace** offers a look at some of Perth's most historic buildings, dating from the 1850s, plus some unusual shopping arcades—notably **London Court**, reminiscent of a quaint Elizabethan-era alley. Elsewhere in Perth, see:

▲▲**Kings Park**, overlooking the west side of downtown. This 1,000-acre expanse, one of Australia's nicest city parks, contains a botanical garden, a restaurant, numerous picnic grounds,

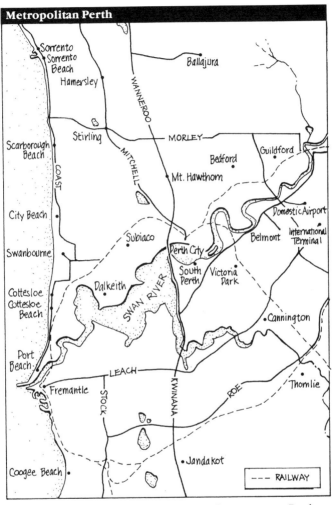

Metropolitan Perth

fountains and memorials, and some grand views across Perth and the Swan River.

▲The **Western Australian Museum,** Francis at Beaufort Street, Northbridge (across the railroad tracks from downtown). It's interesting for its natural antiquities—an 11-ton meteorite, for instance, and a 30-foot whale skeleton. It also has an Aboriginal gallery, wildlife displays and the original 1856 Perth jail.

▲**The Art Gallery of Western Australia**, adjacent to the museum on James Street at Beaufort, shares the Perth Cultural

Centre with the Alexander Library. The $10 million gallery has a superb permanent collection of Australian (especially W.A.) and foreign works, among them Cezanne, Monet, Picasso, Rembrandt, Renoir, Van Gogh and Whistler, plus a fine display of tribal art and regional crafts.

▲▲▲**Swan River cruises** leave from the Barrack Street Jetty at the foot of downtown. **Transperth** offers a 2 p.m. upriver cruise daily (returning at 4:45 p.m.) with an adult fare of A$8; **Captain Cook Cruises** has three-hour daily cruises priced at A$12, leaving at 1:45 p.m. daily; **Golden Swan Cruises** offer full-day excursions to Fremantle for A$33, including lunch and sightseeing, or three-hour afternoon tea cruises for A$12. A fourth operator with trips to Fremantle and upriver to Swan Valley wineries is **Boat Torque Cruises**. Your narrator will point out the Royal Perth Yacht Club, the holder of the America's Cup from 1983 to 1987, and the homes of many of the city's wealthier residents. You'll also see a great many sailboards and other water sports: With no major industry on the river, it is virtually without pollution.

▲▲▲**Beaches** in Perth are among the finest in Australia. Long strands of shimmering white sands extend from the Swan River mouth at North Fremantle for many miles north. Best known, from south to north, are **North Cottesloe**, Prince Charles' personal favorite; Swanbourne, Perth's no. 1 nude beach; City Beach, a family beach with modern facilities; and Scarborough, site of the new $100 million Observation City resort hotel complex.

▲▲**Armadale**, a Perth suburb about 24 km (15 miles) south of downtown, is the home of **Pioneer World**, a recreated working village of the late 19th Century with various merchants and tradesmen, a police station, fire station, general store, schoolhouse, theater and a stream for gold panning. Nearby, you can regress a few more centuries at **The Elizabethan Village** containing replicas of Shakespeare's birthplace and other famous English buildings, plus antique weapons, armor, tapestries and furniture.

Fremantle Sightseeing Highlights

Western Australia's major port, settled in 1829, is situated at the mouth of the Swan River, just 19 km (12 miles) downstream from Perth. At once more historic and more cosmopolitan than its "big brother," it features many 19th Century European-style buildings (more than 150 classified by the National Trust), an active and highly visible artisans' community, and of course its harbor and yachting marina. Fremantle is 35 minutes by Transperth train from downtown Perth; the one-way fare is 55 cents.

▲▲**The Fremantle Museum and Arts Centre**, 1 Finnerty St. at Ord Street, is housed in a handsome stone building constructed in 1860 as a convict lunatic asylum. There are exhibits on the colonial history of Fremantle, the Swan River and the Western Australian coast, plus a fine display of local ceramics, sculpture, textiles, paintings and prints.

▲▲**The Western Australian Maritime Museum**, Cliff Street, exhibits artifacts of W.A.'s rich trading and whaling history. Its star attraction is the *Batavia*, a Dutch sailing vessel shipwrecked in 1629 and now being reassembled timber by timber in the museum.

▲The **America's Cup Museum**, 43 Swan St., North Fremantle, has a collection of model yachts from the first America's Cup race through to the 1987 series, when the swiftest 12-meter sailing boats in the world made their homes in Fremantle for several months. The York Motor Museum of vintage cars is also at this address.

▲▲The **Round House**, on Arthur Head at the west end of High Street, is the state's oldest surviving building. Constructed in 1831 as the Swan River Colony's original civil jail, it affords an excellent view across Fremantle and the harbor. Other convict-era structures include the grim-looking **Fremantle Gaol**, The Terrace (off Fairbairn Street), built by convicts between 1851 and 1859 and still used as a prison; and the **Warder's Quarters** on Henderson Street, stone terrace houses for prison guards and wardens.

▲**Fremantle Markets**, South Terrace and Henderson Street, are a great place to browse for an artsy bargain or indulge in a variety of ethnic foods.

Rottnest Island

Perhaps the biggest surprise of many on this 5-by-11-km (3-by-7-mile) island, 18 km (11 miles) offshore from Fremantle, is that real-estate developers haven't given it a new name. Its present monicker was provided by Dutch Commodore Willen de Vlamingh in 1696 when he mistook the native quokkas, miniature kangaroos, for rats. Developed in the 1830s as a convict farm colony, it was converted to minor resort status in 1917. The **Rottnest Museum**, housed in the 1857 grain-crushing mill, will tell you about the island's historic cottages and natural history. The **Underwater Explorer**, a semi-submersible submarine, offers cruises to look at shipwrecks, marine life and reef formations. But the best way to see the island is to rent a bicycle from **Rottnest Bike Hire**, just behind the Hotel Rottnest, and pay A$5 to pedal around for half a day. (There are no cars on the island.) Visit the salt lakes with their rich bird life, Second World War gun emplacements, a lighthouse on the island's highest point, and impressive sandy beaches inviting you for a swim. You're almost sure to see the friendly little quokkas: the entire island is a wildlife sanctuary.

Get to Rottnest aboard the M/V *Temeraire II* from Barracks Street Jetty in Perth ($18 same-day return) or Fremantle (A$14 return). It's about a 1½-hour ride from Perth. **Boat Torque Cruises** also operate daily package cruises, leaving Perth daily at 9 a.m. (returning at 5:45 p.m.) for A$37 to $42, including lunch at Rottnest and a two-hour bus tour of the island. By air, its A$19 return to Rottnest from the Perth Flight Centre at Perth airport, or A$25 return on the *Island Hopper* helicopter from the Port Beach Road terminal in North Fremantle. Several lodgings are available on the island.

Highlights of Western Australia
Western Australia is Australia's largest state, sprawling across 965,000 square miles from the tropical Kimberley to the forests and meadows of the southwest. Most of it is forboding desert and stark terrain suitable for miners and kangaroos. But there are numerous areas of tourist interest for those with time and inclination.

▲▲**The Southwest** is the state's most fertile region. Besides its orchards, vineyards and cattle farms, there are surfing beaches and limestone caves along the west coast, forests of karri trees (300 feet high, 23 feet around) near Pemberton, the startling bluffs of the **Stirling Range National Park**, and the famous **Wave Rock** near Hyder. The largest towns are **Albany** (pop. 22,000), a beach town and agricultural center; and **Esperance** (pop. 7,000), gateway to the Archipelago of the Recherche, famous among divers. Australians flock to the Southwest in droves between August and November, when spring speckles the meadows and mountain slopes with 8,000 varieties of colorful wildflowers.

▲▲**The Goldfields** district focuses on **Kalgoorlie** (pop. 25,000), center of the state's gold-mining industry, 597 km (371 miles) east of Perth. Not quite a century ago, some 200,000 hopeful "diggers" worked this desert region seeking their fortunes. Kalgoorlie's wide streets and false-fronted hotels today are reminders of the gold-rush era. Travelers visit the Hainault Tourist Mine to learn past and modern gold-mining methods, both under and above ground. Brothels, not legal, are tolerated here. Most of the nearby towns built in the decade following the 1893 discovery of gold—like Gwalia, Broad Arrow and Menzies—are now ghost towns. Alone among them, **Coolgardie** has been preserved as a living monument to the era, although its population has shrunk from 15,000 to 900. Don't miss the **Goldfields Museum**, open daily.

▲▲**The Midlands** include numerous fascinating attractions within a day's drive north and east of Perth. **The Pinnacles**, calcified spires of an ancient forest 30,000 years old, are in Nambung National Park. **New Norcia** is a fragment of medieval Spain, complete with a Benedictine monastery and an astounding museum and art gallery. **York** is the historical (1840s) center of the agriculturally rich Avon Valley.

▲**The North Coast** starts at **Geraldton** (pop. 21,000), a farming and lobster-fishing center 423 km (263 miles) north of Perth. Many famous shipwrecks, including the 1629 *Batavia* disaster, occurred in the Abrolhos isles offshore. A short distance north is the self-proclaimed **Principality of Hutt**, where Prince Leonard, a former farmer with his tongue firmly in cheek, even issues his own postage stamps. **Kalbarri National Park** features some spectacular gorges on the Murchison River. **Carvarvon** (pop. 5,000), 801 km (498 miles) from Perth, is famous for its banana farms and prawning. **Port Hedland** (pop. 12,000), 1547 km (978 miles) from Perth on Highway 1, is the principal port for the Pilbara, Australia's major iron ore region. At nearby Marble Bar, temperatures once exceeded 100 degrees F for five straight months.

▲▲**The Kinberley** is a remote, rugged region best seen during the cool, dry winter season (May to August). **Geikie Gorge**, on the Fitzroy River, and **Windjana Gorge**, on the Meda, are the most remarkable of several grandiose chasms in the King Leopold Ranges. **Tunnel Creek** has gouged a half-mile natural tunnel through limestone. The indented coastline is notable for its prolific crop of crocodiles! (Tourists beware: An American woman was gobbled alive in 1987.) **Broome** (pop. 4,000), 2151 km (1,337 miles) from Perth, is a former pearl-diving center which has shifted its economic base to cultured pearls. Its blend of Europeans with third-generation Japanese, Malays and other Asians is unique in Australia. Northeast of the Kimberley, **Kununurra** (pop. 2,500), 3140 km (1,951 miles) from Perth, was founded in 1960 as a base for the massive Ord River Irrigation Scheme. Water sports and cruises are popular on Lake Argyle, W.A.'s biggest inland body of water. A large diamond mine opened near here in 1985 after a major deposit was discovered.

Helpful Hints

The **Western Australian Tourism Commission** has its offices at 16 St. George's Terrace, Perth (tel. 220-1700. For everyday tourism information and bookings, visit the **Holiday W.A. Centre** at 772 Hay St. in Perth (322-2999) or 4 High St. in Fremantle (tel. 430-5555).

DARWIN AND THE "TOP END"

The main reason to go to Australia's "Top End" —the northern crown of the Northern Territory—is to visit Kakadu National Park. If you saw *Crocodile Dundee* and savored the fantastic wetland wilderness in which most of the Australian segment of the movie was filmed, you know just what Kakadu looks like. You even saw Jabiru, Mick Dundee's "home town," near which park headquarters are located.

Darwin, the gateway to Kakadu, is the hard-drinking capital of the Northern Territory. It has survived Japanese bombing in 1942 and a devastating cyclone in 1974 to become an interesting cosmopolitan city of 65,000.

Your schedule in the "Top End" should allow you a day in Darwin, as much time as you can make available in Kakadu, and possible side trips to Katherine Gorge and/or the Aboriginal communities on Bathurst or Melville islands. Keep in mind, though, that the oppressively humid wet season, from late November through March, is probably not a good time to visit.

Getting There
There are direct daily flights to Darwin from Adelaide, Brisbane, Melbourne, Perth and Sydney aboard Ansett, Ansett W.A. or Australian Airlines, and additional direct flights (not daily) from Cairns, Mount Isa and Port Hedland. Air time from Alice Springs is 1 hour, 50 minutes; from Sydney 4 hours; from Perth (with one stop) 4½ hours. Ansett N.T. offers nonstop flights several times a week to and from Katherine, Tennant Creek and Gove/Nhulunbuy in the Northern Territory. There are also international connections to Indonesia and Singapore.

There's no train service to Darwin, but you can travel overland by private car—a grueling effort, not recommended—or by express coach. No doubt the cheapest way to reach Darwin from major population centers is with an unlimited-mileage bus pass from Ansett Pioneer, Greyhound or Deluxe Coaches. From Alice Springs, buses normally take 21 hours (overnight) and charge A$107.

Getting Around
From Darwin airport, 6 km from town, you can rent a car, take an A$8 taxi ride, or hop on the airport shuttle bus or a A$2.50 ride into downtown. Within the city, public buses (tel. 81-2150) operate 6 a.m. to 11 p.m., Monday to Saturday, at a cost of 30 cents a ride. You can also rent bicycles for A$5 a day at **City Cycle Rental**, 69 Mitchell St. in the Greyhound depot.

You can take a long-distance coach to Katherine, but to Arnhem Land or the offshore Aboriginal reserves, you're best off to book a company tour, of which several are available.

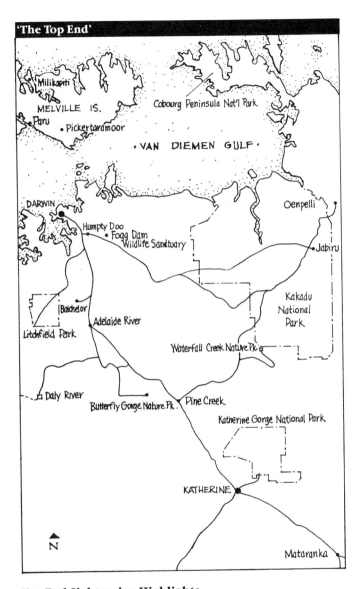

'The Top End'

Milikapiti

MELVILLE IS.

Paru • Pickertaramoor

Cobourg Peninsula Nat'l Park

• VAN DIEMEN GULF •

DARWIN

Oenpelli

Humpty Doo
• Fogg Dam
Wildlife Sanctuary

Jabiru

Batchelor

Kakadu
National
Park

Adelaide River

Litchfield Park

Waterfall Creek Nature Pk.

Daly River

Butterfly Gorge Nature Pk. Pine Creek

Katherine Gorge National Park

N

KATHERINE

Mataranka

Top End Sightseeing Highlights

▲▲**Darwin**, founded in 1869, was named after naturalist Charles Darwin by the captain of H.M.S. *Beagle*, who discovered the harbor 30 years earlier. The main sights include the **Botanical gardens**, established in 1891 and now containing more than 400 species of tropical plants on 85 acres; **Doctor's Gully**, where thousands of ocean fish come in at high tide daily for a free feed of bread; the **Northern Territory Museum of Arts and Natural Sciences**, notable for its primitive art and wildlife exhibits; and the **Artillery Museum**, with reminders of Darwin's World War Two buffeting. If you're up here in June, don't miss the annual **Beer Can Regatta**. Darwinites, who consume an average of 60 gallons of beer per year for every man, woman and child, save up their empty cans for 51 weeks in order to construct an imaginative flotilla that sets sail on Darwin Harbour.

▲▲▲**Kakadu National Park** has been called the greatest wetland remaining on Planet Earth. Over 2,300 square miles in area, it comprises the floodplains of the East, South and West Alligator Rivers and the Wildman River, and the sudden cliffs of the Arnhem Land escarpment with gorges, waterfalls and 18,000-year-old Aboriginal rock paintings. Join a safari for one to eight days of bushwalking, camping and cruising the rivers. After joining one such expedition, my friend Elaine was ecstatic. "Talk about a once in a lifetime experience!" she said. "I saw five crocodiles, water buffalos, kangaroos, dingos, bats and more birds and insects than you can imagine. The place was literally teeming with life." Book a trip from Darwin with **Terra Safari Tours**, 1585 Strath Road, Berrimah, NT (tel. 089/84-3470); **Australian Kakadu Tours**, P.O. Box 1397, Darwin (tel. 81-5144); or **Dial-a-Safari**, 14 Knucky St., Darwin (tel. 81-1244). Costs average around A$100 a day.

▲▲**Bathurst and Melville Islands**, traditional homes of the isolated Tiwi Aboriginal tribes, are situated 80 km (50 miles) north of Darwin across the Clarence Strait. Tiwi pottery and woodcarvings, especially ceremonial grave poles, are unique. Contact **Tiwi Tours**, 27 Temira Crescent, Darwin (tel. 81-5115) to book a highly worthwhile half-day (A$125) or full-day (A$185) tour between March and October.

▲▲**Katherine Gorge National Park**, 31 km (19 miles) from Katherine (pop. 4,500) and 388 km (241 miles) southeast of Darwin, is best known for its boat trips between the sheer, 200-foot-high walls of the chasm. Two-hour cruises run four times daily the rest of the year, for about A$10 adult fare.

Helpful Hints

You'll find the helpful **Northern Territory Government Tourist Bureau** at 31 Smith Street Mall (tel. 81-6611), open 8:45 a.m. to 5 p.m. Monday to Friday and 9 a.m. to noon Saturday.

GREAT BARRIER REEF ISLANDS

If a visit to Green Island (Day 17) whets your appetite for more time in the tropical sun, you'll be pleased to know that there are hundreds of other islands off the coast of Queensland between the Gold Coast and Cape Melville, spread across 1300 km (800 miles) of South Pacific Ocean. Nearly two dozen of them have established resort settlements.

Getting There

The main gateway towns are Bundaberg, Gladstone, Rockhampton, Mackay, Proserpine, Townsville, Cardwell, Tully, Cairns and Cooktown, scattered up the coast north of Brisbane. All are connected by highway; all but Cooktown are linked via rail; all but Cardwell and Tully have domestic airports of their own.

Once you've reached the gateway town, it's a relatively painless procedure to get to the island by boat (every resort has its own launch service from nearby mainland harbors) or small plane. Inquire locally for directions or check with the nearest Queensland Government Travel Centre.

The busiest gateway town is **Proserpine**, the takeoff point for the Whitsunday Islands. Located 1165 km (724 miles) north of Brisbane and 650 km (404 miles) south of Cairns, it is served by nonstop flights from Brisbane, Townsville and Mackay several times a week, and by direct flights (with stops) from Sydney and Melbourne. Coaches connect Proserpine with Shute Harbour, 22 km (14 miles) east, from which launches run several times daily to the various resorts of the Whitsundays.

Island Highlights

Every Barrier Reef island has something a little different to offer the visitor. Some are upscale, jet-set resorts, with all manner of sports facilities and nightlife. Others are limited to rustic cottages or youth hostel accommodations. You're bound to find something to match your desires and price range.

The following listing singles out major resort islands (except for those covered in our Cairns itinerary), starting in the south and moving north:

Lady Elliot Island is the southernmost coral cay on the reef. Visitors come to this tiny isle to enjoy the marine life with tank, snorkel or on foot at low tide. Full board lodging costs A$55 to $75 in scattered cabins or safari tents. There's no launch service; charter aircraft from Bundaberg charge A$95 return.

Heron Island is famous worldwide for its outstanding scuba diving and snorkeling. Just 42 acres in area, this unspoiled cay is surrounded by over 9 square miles of coral reef. The Barrier Reef Divers Festival is held every November; the rest of the year, you can get excellent diving instruction and equipment. In addition to the reef life, you can see green sea turtles and migratory mutton birds nest here (the island is a national park) and lay their eggs in spring and summer. Launches leave Gladstone daily except Thursday at 8 a.m., arriving at Heron Island (a distance of 72 km, or 45 miles) 2 ½ hours later, for A$100 return. Or you can take a helicopter for A$217 return.

Great Keppel Island is as frantic as Heron and Lady Elliot are serene. The largest of 27 mostly-undeveloped islands in the Keppel Group, 13 km (8 miles) east of Yeppoon, near Rockhampton, it is heavily geared toward singles in their 20s. At the main resort, activities are scheduled every minute of the day and night, from water sports to disco dancing (there's a resident rock band), tennis and golf to squash and cricket. The resort is owned by Australian Airlines, which offers weekly packages. To get to Great Keppel, take a coach from Rockhampton to Rosslyn Bay (near Yeppoon), then pay A$12 return for the hydrofoil. There are also several 25-minute flights daily from Rockhampton.

Brampton Island, 32 km (20 miles) north of Mackay, is a national park and wildlife sanctuary. The mountainous, 1,100-acre island is cloaked in tropical forest and surrounded by white sand beaches and coral reefs. It's great for bushwalking among semi-tame kangaroos and colorful lorikeets. At Brampton Island Resort, an Australian Airlines hotel, activities include all manner of water sports, tennis and golf, and a disco for nightlife. Launch service operates daily from Mackay at 9 a.m. The cruise takes an hour, and the cost is A$24 return. If you prefer to fly, Air Queensland makes the short hop from Mackay.

Newry Island, a hilly, wooded national park of just 110 acres, is one of the least known (and most un-touristy) of all the isles off the Queensland coast. Koalas and echidnas are native to the island, a good place for walking and swimming. A small resort accommodates 25 guests; camping is also available. A launch service operates from Victor Creek, 56 km (35 miles) north of Mackay, at 11:00 a.m. every Wednesday, Saturday and Sunday. It takes 15 minutes; the fare is A$10.

Lindeman Island is on the southern fringe of the Whitsunday Group, 74 islands discovered and named by Captain Cook in 1770. Lindeman was the first of the Barrier Reef resorts, established in 1929 and still a favorite for many Australian families. Walking trails climb the hills of this rocky, 2,000-acre isle. There are organized activities for kids of all ages. Launch fare from Shute Harbour is A$20 return; flights from Proserpine are A$60 return.

Hamilton Island is the luxurious, world-class resort center of the Whitsundays. The A$200 million hotel complex features five restaurants and a French bakery, seven bars (including one of the swim-up variety in Australia's largest freshwater pool), an indoor sports complex, a shopping center with four boutiques, a 200-acre fauna park, a 400-boat marina, sport fishing charters and scuba diving instruction, and a "floating hotel," the Coral Cat, hovering above the reef. The 1,200-acre island is quite hilly, but there's enough flat ground for Queensland's only island airport where large jets can land. Ansett flies nonstop daily from Cairns and several times weekly from Brisbane, Sydney and Melbourne. A 45-minute launch service runs twice daily (9 a.m. and 4:45 p.m.) from Shute Harbour for a return fare of A$25.

Long Island has two very different resort communities about 2 km apart. The Ansett-owned Whitsunday 100 Resort competes for the 18-to-35 singles clientele of Great Keppel Island with nonstop water sports by day, disco dancing by night. A$85 to $90 per person. Budget travelers, meanwhile, enjoy Palm Bay Resort, cook their own food (there's a small grocery) and enjoy bush walking and snorkeling. Long Island is a lush national park 11 km (7 miles) long, no more than 1½ km wide, and everywhere mountainous. Launches run four times daily (9 a.m. to 4:45 p.m.) from Shute Harbour, 8 km (5 miles) northwest. The round-trip fare is A$16 to Palm Bay, A$20 to Whitsunday 100.

South Molle Island is a 1,000-acre island of steep bush-covered hills and coral-fringed bays in the heart of the Whitsunday Passage. A national park, it is criss-crossed by walking tracks and inhabited by brightly colored lorikeets. The medium-sized resort offers water sports, fishing, gymnasium, golf and tennis. It is served by restaurants, bars and other facilities. Launch service from Shute Harbour (daily at 9 a.m., 1 and 5 p.m.) costs A$20 return.

Daydream Island is tiny, just ¾ of a mile long and barely 500 metres (547 yards) wide. Social life on this speck of paradise, clutched by white coral beaches and lazy coconut palms, focuses on the resort's huge lagoon-style swimming pool with its bar on a central island (no "dry" martinis here). There are the usual variety of water and other sports, and a disco for night. The island is served twice daily (9 a.m. and 5 p.m.) by launch from Shute Harbour, 5 km (3 miles) distant, for A$15 return.

Hayman Island, one of the oldest of the Reef resorts (it dates from the 1950s), was reincarnated in 1986 as a five-star resort after a A$100 million renovation by Ansett. It's a universally appealing island with 1,000 acres of rugged mountain scenery, a wide fringe of reef, palm-shaded beaches, and dozens of species of birds and butterflies. The Ansett International Hotel has five restaurants, a library, a lively entertainment center and fine water sports facilities. If you aren't in the mood for a cruise

boat from Shute Harbour (A$25 return), you can fly by
helicopter from Proserpine or direct by Turbo Beaver from
Airlie Beach (near Shute Harbour) or Townsville.

Magnetic Island is almost a suburb of Townsville. Just 13 km
(8 miles) north of Queensland's third largest city, it attracts hundreds or even thousands of day trippers. But it's big
enough—20 square miles—that the throngs are easily escaped.
Another mountainous national park island, it has fine bush
walking, a fernery and an aquarium, bird and koala sanctuaries,
two dozen sandy beaches and a motor road linking several
resort villages along the eastern shore. (The island even has its
own bus service.) You can rent bicycles or mopeds at Picnic
Bay, where the ferry arrives 8 to 12 times daily from Townsville
(35 minutes, A$6 return). The island contains at least a half-
dozen official and unofficial youth hostels, numerous holiday flats
and economy-priced hotels in Picnic Bay and Arcadia. Australian Airlines' Alma Dean Beach Resort midway up the east
coast is a top resort.

Orpheus Island is one of the more secluded of the reef
resorts, 80 km (50 miles) northwest of Townsville and 24
km (15 miles) east of Lucinda, near Ingham. Eleven km (7 miles)
long, not quite a mile wide, and fringed with reef, the forested
island—volcanic in origin—is a national park rich in birdlife
and turtle nesting grounds. There's no regular launch service,
but seaplanes or helicopters operate daily from Townsville for
A$155 return.

Hinchinbrook Island is the world's largest island national park,
a 144-square-mile Tahitian landscape of lush rainforest, mist-
shrouded mountains (up to 3,400 feet high), spectacular waterfalls, rocky caves, sandy beaches (on the east coast) and rich
wildlife. A narrow channel separates it from the mainland east
of Cardwell, about halfway between Townsville and Cairns.
Launches leave Cardwell daily except Monday at 9 a.m., with a
fare of A$24 return.

Bedarra Island is a tiny and exclusive resort island. One mile
long and a half-mile wide, four miles off the coast near Tully, it
is densely forested and ringed by white sandy beaches. The
new Bedarra Bay Resort consists of two dozen elaborate guest
bungalows set in a tropical garden along the ocean. There's no
organized entertainment of any type—nothing but "intimate,
casual and elegant" relaxation, as promoters put it. No one
under 15 is allowed. Reach Bedarra aboard a daily launch service via Dunk Island from Clump Point, near Tully (A$18
return).

Dunk Island is another unspoiled gem with a remarkably rich
fauna and flora. Lush jungle caresses the slopes of 900-foot
Mount Koo-tal-oo, providing a home for some 150 species of

birds, plus dozens of beetles and butterflies, lizards and snakes, bats and echidnas. The island is only 520 acres in size, but it somehow seems larger. Sophisticated over-30s like its Great Barrier Reef Hotel, which offers all the sports of other island resorts plus horseback riding, skeet shooting and nature activities. Get there on a launch from Clump Point, 5 km (3 miles) west, for A$12 return; water taxi from South Mission Beach; or a flight with Australian Airlines (the resort owner) daily from Townsville and several times a week from Cairns.

Lizard Island is the northernmost of the Barrier Reef resort islands, 95 km (59 miles) northeast of Cooktown. Situated close to the magnificent outer reef, this lovely 4-square-mile island has great beaches, better snorkeling, and some of the world's finest big-game fishing within easy cast. Lizard Island Lodge is an exclusive resort overlooking a coral lagoon. Air Queensland flies to Lizard Island at least once a day from Cairns (A$96) or Cooktown (A$58).

Helpful Hints

Queensland Government Travel Centres are situated in three towns between Brisbane and Cairns: Rockhampton (119 East St., tel. 079/27-8611); Mackay (River Street, tel. 079/57-2292); and Townsville (303 Flinders Mall, tel. 077/71-3077). The AGTC's main office is at 196 Adelaide St., Brisbane, Qld. 4000 (tel. 07/31-2211). Most of the reef resorts have postal service and shops; many also have banking facilities and resident medical practitioners.

HOLIDAYS & FESTIVALS

January
New Year's Day (1st)
Australia Day (1st Monday after Jan. 26)
Surfing carnivals (throughout beach communities until March)

February
Festival of Perth (1st three weeks)

March
Moomba Festival, Melbourne (10 days early in month)
Festival of Arts, Adelaide (even-numbered years)
Hunter Valley Vintage Festival, New South Wales
Sheffield Shield Final, national cricket championship

April
Barossa Vintage Festival, South Australia, odd-numbered years
Festival of the Rocks, Sydney (week before Easter)
Good Friday and Easter Sunday (dates vary)
Royal Agricultural Show, Sydney (Easter week)
ANZAC Day (25th)

May
Bangtail Muster, Alice Springs (first weekend)

June
Beer Can Regatta, Darwin (1st weekend)
Townsville Pacific Festival (11 days in early June)
Queen's Birthday (2nd Monday, except in W.A.)

July
Lots of footy and horse races, if nothing else

August
Brisbane Royal Show (middle of month)
Shinju Matsuri, Broome, W.A. (3rd through 4th weekend)
Henley-on-Todd Regatta, Alice Springs (last Saturday)
Australian Ski Championships, Thredbo

September
Royal Adelaide Show (early in month)
Melbourne Royal Agricultural Show (middle of month)
Spoleto Festival of Arts, Melbourne (last two weeks)
Warana Spring Carnival, Brisbane (last two weeks)
Victorian Football League Grand Final, Melbourne (4th Saturday)

October
Perth Royal Show (early in month)
Queen's Birthday (1st Monday, W.A. only)
Tropicarnival, Gold Coast (2nd week)
Royal Hobart Show (3rd weekend)
Australian Formula 1 Grand Prix, Adelaide (end of month)

November
Melbourne Cup horse race (1st Tuesday)
Australian Open Golf Tournament (3rd weekend)

December
Christmas and Boxing Day (Dec. 25 and 26)
Sydney-to-Hobart Yacht Race (starting Dec. 26)

JMP TRAVELERS CATALOG

All Items Field Tested, Highly Recommended, Completely Guaranteed and Discounted Below Retail.

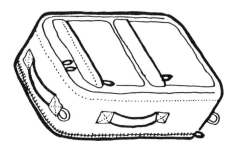

Combination Rucksack/
Suitcase . . . . $70.00 postpaid

At 9″ x 21″ x 13″, this specially designed, sturdy, functional bag is maximum carry-on-the-plane size. (Fits under the seat.) Constructed by Jesse Ltd. of rugged waterproof nylon Cordura material, with hide-away shoulder straps, waist belt (for use as a ruck sack) and top and side handles and a detachable shoulder strap (for toting as a suitcase). Perimeter zippers allow easy access to the roomy (2200 cu. in.) central compartment. Two small outside pockets are perfect for maps and other frequently used items. Two thousand JMP Travelers took these bags around the world last year and returned satisfied. Comparable bags cost much more. If you're looking for maximum "carry-on size" and a suitcase that can be converted into a back pack, this is your best bet. Available in navy blue, black, gray or burgundy.

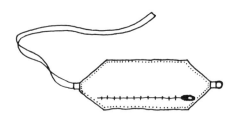

Money Belt . . . . $8.95 postpaid

Required! Ultra-light, sturdy, under-the-pants, nylon pouch just big enough to carry the essentials comfortably. We never travel without one and hope you won't either. Beige, nylon zipper, one size fits all, with instructions.

Qty.	Title	Each	Total
	Alaska in 22 Days - *Lanier* (March '88)	$ 6.95	
	American Southwest in 22 Days - *Harris* (April '88)	6.95	
	Australia in 22 Days - *Gottberg*	6.95	
	China in 22 Days - *Duke & Victor*	6.95	
	Europe in 22 Days - *Steves*	6.95	
	Germany, Austria & Switzerland in 22 Days - *Steves*	6.95	
	Great Britain in 22 Days - *Steves*	6.95	
	India in 22 Days - *Mathur* (April '88)	6.95	
	Japan in 22 Days - *Old*	6.95	
	Mexico in 22 Days - *Rogers & Rosa*	6.95	
	Norway, Denmark & Sweden in 22 Days - *Steves*	6.95	
	West Indies in 22 Days - *Morreale*	6.95	
	All-Suite Hotel Guide - *Lanier*	9.95	
	Asia 101 - *Gottberg* (March '88)	11.95	
	Asia Through the Back Door - *Steves & Gottberg*	11.95	
	Complete Guide to Bed & Breakfasts - *Lanier*	12.95	
	Elegant Small Hotels - *Lanier*	12.95	
	Europe 101 - *Steves*	11.95	
	Europe Through the Back Door - *Steves*	11.95	
	Gypsying After 40 - *Harris*	12.95	
	Heart of Jerusalem - *Nellhaus* (Feb. '88)	12.95	
	Mona Winks - *Steves* (April '88)	9.95	
	People's Guide to Camping in Mexico - *Franz* (April '88)	11.95	
	People's Guide to Mexico - *Franz*	13.95	
		Subtotal	$
		Shipping	$ 1.75
		Total enclosed	$

Non-U.S. payments must be in
U.S. funds drawn on a U.S. bank.

METHOD OF PAYMENT (CHECK ONE)

☐ Charge to my (circle one): MasterCard   VISA   AmEx
☐ Check or Money Order Enclosed (Sorry, no CODs or Cash)
Credit Card Number

Expiration Date ☐☐ — ☐☐

Signature _____
               Required for Credit Card Purchases
Telephone: Office (___)_____ Home (___)_____
Name _____
Address _____
City _____ State _____ Zip _____

Send to: John Muir Publications
P.O. Box 613   Santa Fe, NM 87504-0613
(505) 982-4078
Please allow 4-6 weeks for delivery.